SECOND EDITION

Classroom

ACTIVATORS

*I would like to dedicate this book to my wife,
Mary, and my two lovely daughters, Julia and Emily.*

SECOND EDITION

Classroom
ACTIVATORS

More Than **100** Ways to Energize Learners

Jerry Evanski

CORWIN
PRESS
A SAGE Company

For information:

Corwin Press
A SAGE Company
2455 Teller Road
Thousand Oaks, California 91320
www.corwinpress.com

SAGE Ltd.
1 Oliver's Yard
55 City Road
London EC1Y 1SP
United Kingdom

SAGE India Pvt. Ltd.
B 1/I 1 Mohan Cooperative
  Industrial Area
Mathura Road, New Delhi
India 110 044

SAGE Asia-Pacific Pte. Ltd.
33 Pekin Street #02-01
Far East Square
Singapore 048763

Printed in the United States of America

Library of Congress Cataloging-in-Publication Data

Evanski, Jerry.
Classroom activators: more than 100 ways to energize learners /
Jerry Evanski. —2nd ed.
    p. cm.
Includes bibliographical references and index.
ISBN 978-1-4129-6881-2 (cloth)
ISBN 978-1-4129-6882-9 (pbk.)
    1. Effective teaching. 2. Motivation in education.
3. Learning—Social aspects. I. Title.

LB1025.3.E865 2009
371.3—dc22   2008020255

This book is printed on acid-free paper.

09   10   11   12   10   9   8   7   6   5   4   3   2   1

Acquisitions Editor:	Cathy Hernandez
Associate Editor	Desirée A. Bartlett
Editorial Assistant:	Ena Rosen
Production Editor:	Libby Larson
Copy Editor:	Taryn Bigelow
Typesetter:	C&M Digitals (P) Ltd.
Proofreader:	Ellen Brink
Graphic Designer:	Scott Van Atta

Contents

Acknowledgments

The ideas and inspirations in this book came from many sources. I would like to thank Bobbi DePorter; Eric Jensen; John LeTellier; Rich Allen; Jean Blaydes; Karen Borbolla; Dana Marino and Educational Resources Network; the Brain-Based Learning cohorts at Oakland University, Rochester, Michigan; Dr. Ron Spalter; Elsie Ritzenhein; and the staff and students at Erie Elementary School, Chippewa Valley School District, Clinton Township, Michigan.

Corwin Press gratefully acknowledges the contributions of the following individuals:

Patricia Allanson, Seventh Grade Math Teacher
Deltona Middle School
Deltona, FL

Carol Amos, Grades K–6 Math Teacher
Twinfield Union School
Wheelock, VT

Sherri Becker, Educational Technology Integrationist
Mitchell School District
Mitchell, SD

Pamela Nevills, Teacher Supervisor
University of California, Riverside
Riverside, CA

Delise Teague, Instructional Coach
McNairy County School System
Selmer, TN

Linda Winburn, Instructional Coach
Richland District Two
Columbia, SC

About the Author

 Dr. Jerry Evanski has been a teacher and school administrator at all levels K–12. He has written several books and has taught at the university level for many years. Dr. Evanski received his bachelor's degree in music from Michigan State University, East Lansing, Michigan, and received a master's degree in music education, and an educational specialist and doctorate degree in general administration and supervision from Wayne State University, Detroit, Michigan. He has been conducting workshops nationally and internationally for Discipline Associates and for the Teacher Learning Center for the past two decades. He created and teaches the Brain-Based Learning certification program at Oakland University in Rochester, Michigan. The video he created about the program won two Telly Awards. He is also a trained facilitator for Super Camp, which is an internationally known accelerated learning program. His current research is focused on identifying and correcting potential visual, auditory, and kinesthetic blocks to learning.

Introduction

BRAIN RESEARCH AND THE CLASSROOM

The abundance of brain research available to educators at this stage in history is staggering. For the first time in history, the human brain can be observed as it is actually functioning, providing hard data on how the brain learns and remembers best. Educators now have the opportunity to make instructional decisions not based on philosophy or personal experience, but on objective data. This book is filled with these neuroscience findings, and practical applications of them in the classroom.

Getting the Input Put In

Much of the research being done on the brain has absolutely nothing to do with education. The research that does have to do with educational topics must be viewed carefully. It is a big leap from the neuron to the neighborhood. Research could take place at the systems level, all the way down to the individual neurons, to even the cell membranes and the synaptic gap. To make a leap of logic and apply research done at a microscopic level to a first-grade classroom or a tenth-grade chemistry class must be undertaken cautiously.

With that note of caution, I strongly urge all educators to take that step. Primary research reports are easy to find on the World Wide Web. As educators in this most exciting time, we must be bold and always have some action research project in the works, to make that leap from the neuron to the neighborhood in a practical way.

This book is a result of one such leap. I believe that the first phase in learning is getting the information inside the students' heads, or as I like to put it, "Getting the Input Put In." Research has helped to find the best ways to do just that.

A necessary step before that, however, is to get the students' attention so the input can be put in. If a lesson doesn't get into the brain to be processed in the first place, then the information doesn't have any chance of being transferred into long-term memory.

One important question educators should ask is, "How long can our students pay attention?" The time frame varies from shorter to longer, depending on several factors. These factors may include the time of day, student interest level in the topic, the energy and expertise of the instructor, how the students are feeling, how hungry they are, and a host of other variables (Burns, 1985; Johnstone & Percival, 1976). In addition, the ability to pay attention for longer periods may be compromised by environmental factors such as extensive early exposure to television (Christakis, Zimmerman, DiGiuseppe, & McCarty, 2004). So how long can today's students pay attention? Without being glib, I think the answer is "not as long as they used to be able to, and not as long as we would like."

Are Kids' Brains Different?

Why do I make the statement that kids today can't pay attention as long as they used to? Are we teaching to different brains than we were 20 or 30 years ago? Well, not exactly. The point must be made that the brains of kids today are exactly the same as the brains of kids 30 years ago. Kids' brains today still have four lobes, still are made up of neurons and glial cells, and they still change when they interact with the environment.

So, physically, students have the same brains as students 30 years ago. How that brain is organized, however, is radically different in students in today's world. It is similar to saying automobiles from the 1960s are the same as automobiles today. They still have tail lights, steering wheels, and brakes, but because the environment has changed and style has changed, the cars are radically different.

The brain inside the head of today's student has been shaped by the radically different environment of today, and as a result, has in fundamental ways been wired differently from the brain of 20 to 30 years ago. My speculation is that 20 or 30 years from now, brains will be different still. How can I make such a strong statements, and what can educators do about it? The answer lies in the amazing research that has been done with the human brain.

Since the late 1960s, thanks to the pioneering work of Dr. Marian Diamond, we know about *brain plasticity*, the idea that the brain changes as a result of interacting with the environment. If we know that the brain changes through interactions with the environment, the other relevant question is whether the environment has changed since we ourselves were students.

I believe the answer to that question is a resounding yes. The environment has changed more in the past 20 to 30 years than perhaps at any other time in history. This was underscored during a recent visit with my eight-year-old daughter to a well-known chain electronics store. At one point, we stopped shopping and I told my daughter to look around. It occurred to me at that moment that although she thought the store and its merchandise were very ordinary, this was a most extraordinary store. It was extraordinary because most of the store's merchandise did not exist in any form when I was my daughter's age. We looked at personal computers, PalmPilots, DVDs, video players, flat-screen televisions, microwaves, pocket calculators, cell phones . . . the list goes on and on with these new technologies that were not available a few decades ago, but have now become such a part of contemporary life.

When I was young, we played with jump ropes and board games and passed notes in class. Students today play video games, surf the World Wide Web, and IM each other. Physical safety is a priority today, resulting in car seats with five-point restraints and playgrounds that are much more static than they once were. Not much moves besides the swings. Moving equipment, like teeter totters and spinning carousels, has been removed because of liability issues. Children today, however, are more often exposed to drugs, ranging from caffeine to antidepressants, at a very young age. Many leisure-time activities of today's students are isolated affairs, as they interact with the video display, computer screen, or television, often more than with other children.

So, the environment has changed. And when the environment changes, the brains in contact with the environment have different connections. How do we get and keep the attention of this different brain that has been raised on microprocessors and cell phones?

Research indicates a direction for specific techniques to assist teachers in getting and keeping the attention of today's youth. This book is filled with scores of ideas to get and keep such students' attention.

So what is it that research is suggesting? A few times an hour—maybe more, maybe less, depending on your students, their interest level, the time of day, and so on—I recommend that you engage your students in something called a *state change*, to refresh their ability to pay attention and address their physiological needs.

State Change

The textbook definition of a state change is that it is "a holistic phenomenon of mind-body emotions, mood, emotional condition; sum total of all neurological and physical processes within an individual at any moment in time" (Hall & Belnap, 2002, p. xx). A friendlier definition is that a state change is a change in a student's thoughts, feelings, or physiology. This book lists specific directions for how to incorporate state changes that last from a few seconds to a few minutes, or more.

For those readers who think state changes have to be complicated to be effective, I offer the following story:

The Story of the King

A long time ago in a different land, there lived a king who had three sons, all of whom he loved very much. He could not decide which one to leave his vast fortune to, so he proposed a challenge. One day, he gathered his three sons together outside an immense storehouse at the back of the palace grounds. The king gave each of his sons a portion of the fortune, and showed them the inside of the storehouse, which had been emptied. He told them that the challenge was to spend the riches he had just given them on whatever they wished, but the task was to fill up the immense storehouse to the ceiling.

The first son immediately went out and spent his part of the fortune on dirt, because it was cheap. Amazingly, he managed to purchase enough soil to fill the storehouse over halfway, but, as his father pointed out, not to the ceiling.

The second son spent his money on hay and straw, and managed to fill the storehouse almost two-thirds of the way to the ceiling, but, again, had fallen short of the goal.

When the storehouse had again been emptied, the last son took his father to the storehouse at twilight. Just as evening was gently wrapping the palace up with shadows, he asked his father to step inside. Once inside the storehouse, the son shut the door, leaving the two of them briefly in darkness. Then the son pulled from his tunic a single candle, lit it, and filled the storehouse to the ceiling with . . . light.

The moral to the story is that state changes do not have to be complex, expensive, or lengthy to be effective.

So far I have suggested regularly doing state changes, and I have acknowledged that state changes can be very simple and very quick and still be effective. I'd like to make two additional points about state changes—the importance of gradient and the need to adopt and adapt.

Gradient

Gradient is simply the risk factor involved in any activity. Some of the activities presented here are so low risk that in my experience, very few if any students refuse to participate. Some of the activities suggested, in particular those in the last section, could be higher gradient, that is, have a higher risk involved, than other activities. A mistake I made early in my career was to not consider gradient at all. Instead, I just tried to have the class do whatever energizing activity I had just learned or heard about. Sometimes it worked, but many times the hoped-for increase in energy and attention eluded me. Now I know that while my directions were good and the activity was strong, the gradient was just too high at that stage of my relationship with those classes.

My suggestion is to set yourself up for success. Read through the activities with your class in mind and choose ones you feel confident the class will participate in and enjoy. As the students begin to get in the rhythm of regular state changes, my experience has been that they will be more open to trying more involved state changes.

Adopt and Adapt

I have used all of these activities with elementary-aged students through adults. If you find one that you like, but you don't think it will work with your particular group, I encourage you to first *adopt* the idea that state changes are useful, even *essential*, to an optimal classroom experience, and *adopt* the notion that having fun is vital for best possible classroom atmosphere and for everyone's mental and emotional well-being, then *adapt* a particular activity for your particular class or teaching situation.

With any luck, the foundational spirit of fun, laughter, joy, and spontaneity come through loud and clear in the spirit of this book and the ideas contained within.

USING THIS BOOK

Our brains basically "run on empty." The human brain does not store energy. The brain needs a constant blood supply, which brings it oxygen and nutrients. Many of the state changes presented here are designed to energize students, and get their blood full of oxygen and flowing to the brain.

These state changes come from a wide range of resources and fields, many of them from outside of education. Contained within these pages you will find activities inspired by such diverse fields as occupational therapy, vision therapy, and sensory integration therapy.

Some of the activities can be done individually; some are designed to do in a group. The group activities can have the added advantage of creating a feeling of bonding in a team or classroom community, which is essential for creating a safe, threat-free environment where all can learn.

I encourage you to keep this book at your fingertips, and when a state change is required, turn to one and try it out. You could also select state changes in advance for use during a particular class or semester.

I have reorganized the state changes around the following four themes:

✦ Energize the Environment
✦ Get Your Students' Attention
✦ Energize Your Students
✦ Build Teams and Community

The first part, "Energize the Environment," examines numerous ways to keep the learning environment fresh.

The second part, "Get Your Students' Attention," is full of ideas to help students focus on the task at hand, an essential first step in the learning process.

The third part, "Energize Your Students," is full of ideas you can use when the students just need a little bit of a state change to refresh their attentional systems in the middle of a lesson.

The last section, "Build Teams and Community," has activities that you could use for an extended state change, and also for community building, team building, and rapport building.

Another feature of this new edition is the inclusion of a suggested age range for each activity; however, I have used every single one of these activities with students of all ages, from kindergarten to post-graduate level, with some adaptations for age, body size, attention span, and so forth. So, if you see an activity you may be interested in that you think your kids would never go for, I would suggest you go back to the team building section and try some of those activities. For me, whenever I have succeeded in the facilitation of a classroom community, anything goes!

The designations for the activities will be as follows:

K–Adult = can be a successful activity for all ages

K–Grade 2 = lower elementary

Grades 3–5 = upper elementary

Grades 6–8 = middle school

Grades 9–12 = high school

Adult = college and beyond

The label K–Adult indicates that any age, kindergarten through adult, will benefit from the activity. That may not necessarily mean, however, that the state change should be used exactly as written for each age level. Please feel free to adapt an activity to the age level, maturity level, and space and time available. You know, do what teachers do!

HOW AND WHEN TO USE THESE ACTIVITIES

Your students will let you know when they need a state change. You could do an activity that gives you a feel for how energized your class is as a whole, such as "One-Word Whip," described in the section on Get Your Students' Attention. Students may ask you for a break. Usually, they will be more subtle than that, but they do give many clues.

What kind of clues do students provide to let you as the teacher know that it is time for a state change? Well, perhaps as you are teaching, their gaze may start to wander or they may look at the clock. They may get fidgety, noisy, and restless. They may ask to use the restroom or get a drink or retrieve something from their locker. Student body language also gives out clues. The body and the brain are connected. Whatever happens in the body (thirsty, uncomfortable, restless) affects the brain, and whatever is happening in the brain (bored, need a break, need to move) affects the body and shows up as a clue that a state change is needed. Maybe your students slump in their chairs, or rest their head on their hands, or put their head down, and so on.

Once you tune in, the clues become more obvious. But when do you do a state change? And how can you get students refocused after a state change? To answer the first question, I recommend that you use state changes in the following four ways:

1. As part of the lesson.

2. As a "parenthesis" in the lesson.

3. As part of the classroom rituals and routines.

4. During natural breaks in the lesson.

As Part of the Lesson

I have used state changes in several ways. One way is to implement a state change that also keeps the learning episode going (See the "Feedback" section in Get Your Students' Attention for some ideas). For example, if I am lecturing, I may see the students need a state change by the way they are looking around the room, getting restless, or by the way their body language is telling me they are losing interest (slumped in chairs, holding head up with hands, etc.). In that case, I may choose to stop my lecture, have students stand, find a partner, and discuss one aspect of what I was just lecturing on. This serves the dual purpose of being a change of state, and helping the learning along by having students actively process information in an interactive way.

As a "Parenthesis" in the Lesson

I could also pause the instruction and insert a very brief state change that has nothing to do with the current lesson. For example, in a high school classroom, I might say, "OK, ladies and gentlemen, put your pens down for a moment and please stand up. Our brains need a steady supply of blood to bring in oxygen and nutrients. We have great blood pumps in our bodies. Our heart is the best, and another blood pump we have is our calf muscles. Please do a few toe lifts [instructor demonstrates]. Great. Take a deep breath; now blow it out. Take another deep breath and as you blow it out, sit down. Now, the process of mitosis is . . ." and back to the lecture.

As Part of the Classroom Rituals and Routines

There are natural points in the flow of a lesson where a state change could be inserted as part of your ritual and routine in class. For example, breathing every time you turn the page of a text (see the "Breathing" section in Part 2, Get Your Students' Attention for more ideas).

During Natural Breaks in the Lesson

There are also natural breaks in the flow of a lesson where a state change could be inserted, for example, when transitioning from lecture to beginning homework, when going from whole group to partners, and so on.

REFOCUSING STUDENTS AFTER A STATE CHANGE

Most often I do a physical state change that doesn't have anything to do with the particular content I am teaching. When it's completed, I simply go back to where I was in the lesson. I have rarely had much difficulty getting students to focus again; actually, the opposite is true. If I do not do a state change at the appropriate time, it seems extremely difficult to get students to continue paying attention once they have checked out.

Please enjoy these activities—they are all shared with you in the hope that they will help your students, and help you be the absolute best, life-changing-force-of-nature teacher you can be—and have an absolutely outrageously fun time doing it!

PART 1

Energize the Environment

THE RIGHT STUFF

Our area of clear vision comes from a small area in the back of each of our eyes called the macula. The rest of our vision is all peripheral vision. In the periphery of our vision, we are unconsciously aware of many aspects of the environment that could help us pay attention and get the input put in, or could detract from our ability to pay attention to the content being taught. If I have students who have trouble paying attention, lack focus, or may not be interested in my content, I must work hard every class period to make sure that everything I can control in my environment is as congruent as possible to meet my end goal, which is to have the students learn.

⊙ Clutter

(K–Adult)

If you are a teacher who leaves stacks of paper leaning on every counter and your desk, I could say, "Hey, that's your style" and not argue the point. Besides, you would just tell me you know where everything is anyway. I used to be a bit like that; but after learning about the power of the environment, and after being convinced that everything in my classroom says something about the kind of learning I expect and the kind of teacher I am, I have cleaned up my act, literally. If there is even a little attention being paid by some students to the pile of papers on my counter, and if they wonder even for a moment if and when the stack will fall, then I have lost that bit of their attention to my content.

To combat this, I suggest looking around the room and noticing what is out of place. At first, it may seem a little obsessive, but after a while, it becomes a habit that is worth the time you invest. Are the chairs out of line? Are the window shades in your room at different heights? Are the hangers on your coat rack jumbled together, or neatly spaced? Are the posters in the room and on the bulletin board hung evenly? Are the papers stacked uniformly? All of this and more can be accomplished by you and your students in a few minutes in the morning, or in a few moments at the end of every class.

◎ Just Hanging Around

(K–Adult)

Many teachers hang student work and projects from the ceiling. My issue with this is that every time the air conditioner comes on in the classroom, the papers will move. Not only will the student with ADHD look, but so will every kid with that paper in their peripheral vision. It's what I call a *biological imperative*. Our visual system sends most of the incoming visual signal to the back of the brain, to the occipital lobe. Some incoming information, however, gets sent right down to the brain stem. Our brains are constantly monitoring incoming information to see if it is harmful or helpful to us. If we see movement in our peripheral vision, our instinct is to look to check it to determine if this stimulus represents a threat. After a while, we will become attuned to it and not look, but why put up with a potential competitor for your students' sometimes-fragile attention, even for a minute? My advice would be to reduce or eliminate distracting movement in your classroom.

LIGHTING

Our brains are hardwired to pay attention to novel stimuli. This may be a survival instinct, to alert us to anything new in the environment that could be a potential hazard. Educators can take advantage of this and increase their students' awareness and attention by varying the type, amount, and location of lighting in a classroom.

Lighting is one of the more studied aspects of educational environments. The type of lighting used in classrooms may have a positive impact on student depression or on short-term and long-term memory and problem solving (Tithof, 1998). An extensive study involving 21,000 students revealed that exposure to natural sunlight positively affected academic performance. Those students exposed to the most natural light during the day progress 15 percent faster in math and 23 percent faster in reading than students in classrooms with the least amount of sunlight (Heschong Mahone Group, 1999). Consider taking into account some of the following ideas about lighting, to keep your classroom environment invigorating.

☺ Manipulate Away!

(K–Adult)

Manipulate the amount, quality, and kind of light in your classroom.

✦ If you are reading a dramatic or emotional piece, shut off several banks of lights to enhance the mood.
✦ Use dramatic lighting to tell a story. Use the overhead projector as a spotlight; shine a flashlight under your chin to light your face. (Remember telling scary stories around a campfire?)

✦ Have a question/answer session with the lights off, pointing at participants with a flashlight when it is their turn to respond.

✦ Use table lamps instead of overhead fluorescent lighting.

✦ Experiment with different colors of light bulbs for the holidays. Try a green bulb for Saint Patrick's Day or a red bulb for Valentine's Day.

✦ Try using some full-spectrum light bulbs. Research on the effects of full-spectrum light on students include findings that seem to indicate that students who learn under full-spectrum light may learn faster, test higher, grow faster, have fewer absences, and even have fewer cavities (Hathaway, Hargreaves, Thompson, & Novitsky, 1992)!

THE SENSE OF SMELL

Our sense of smell is unique among our senses in that it is the only sense that directly connects to our limbic system, where our brain houses structures such as the amygdala and the hippocampus, which are responsible for processing emotions and memory.

Interestingly, the molecules that make up the essential oils used in aromatherapy are among the few molecules that can pass through the blood-brain barrier, which is a densely packed lining of cells that protects the brain from harmful chemicals.

Only after the incoming sensory information has passed through the limbic system does the information arrive in the higher cortical brain regions for perception and interpretation. Our sense of smell has a direct link, indeed, the most direct link, between incoming sensory information and emotions and memory.

Researchers are well aware of this link, and the research on aromas is far-reaching and has shown some amazing effects.

For example, aromas have been shown to reduce dental pain, reduce anxiety, and improve moods (Lehrner, Marwinski, Lehr, Johren, & Deecke, 2005).

Aromas also can lower anxiety (Burnett, Solterbeck, & Strapp, 2004), reduce postpartum depression (Imura, Misao, & Ushijima, 2006), lessen dysmenorrhea (menstrual cramps, pain, and discomfort) (Han, Hur, Buckle, Choi, & Lee, 2006), and help to alleviate insomnia (Lewith, Godfrey, & Prescott, 2005).

◎ Fresh Aromas

(K–Adult)

In the classroom, I am not that interested in reducing dental pain; however, I would love to find ways to increase the state of arousal in my students, to lower their anxiety, and to improve their memory. After making certain that no students have any sensitivities or allergies to any aromas, I suggest you get a book on aromatherapy, a nice air diffuser, and some essential oils to try to enhance the environment in your classroom.

+ Try rosemary or mandarin oil to increase your students' alertness.
+ Rosemary and sage have positive effects on memory.
+ Lavender has positive effects on student mood, making them less depressed, more relaxed (Diego et al., 1998).
+ The use of brandy mint and lavender has been shown to decrease fatigue (Leshchinskaia, Makarchuk, Lebeda, Krivenko, & Sgibnev, 1983).

◎ Easy Enhancements

(K–Adult)

If you don't want to get all fancy with the essential oils, our sense of smell is still an amazing, and perhaps underutilized, sense in our classrooms. Maybe try some of the low-tech ideas listed below to enhance your classroom:

✦ Pop fresh popcorn when beginning a new unit or reviewing for a test. Pop some more during the test.

✦ Once in a while, put potpourri on your desk or on the students' desks.

✦ Sprinkling a little powered deodorizer on the carpet will freshen the scent of the room.

✦ Try a plug-in room deodorizer for the addition of a pleasant odor in your classroom.

THE EFFECTS OF IONS

Ionized air occurs naturally around waterfalls, ocean waves, and rainstorms. This is one reason the air can smell fresh and invigorating after a rainstorm. Numerous studies have shown the positive effects negative ions in the air can have on mood and performance. Cognitive experiments conducted with rats can be a valid predictor of what happens to humans under similar conditions, because the brain of a rat (actually the brain of any mammal) has the same basic building blocks that human brains have, that is, neurons and glial cells. Thus, predictions can be made about human behavior from rat studies. One experiment conducted with rats (Duffee & Koontz, 1965) showed a 350 percent improvement in cognitive functioning on a water-maze performance task when exposed to negative ions.

There are also many negative ion experiments that have been conducted on humans. One study, done in England (Hawkins & Barker, 1978), showed that there were significant increases in people's ability to perform cognitive tasks when exposed to negatively ionized air. A study was even conducted to see if ionized air could improve memory and attention in students with learning disabilities (Morton & Kershner, 1984). The study showed that all of the children breathing negatively ionized air were superior in incidental memory. The results showed enhanced performance on the order of 8.4 percent for students without learning disabilities, and an almost 24 percent improvement in performance on memory tasks for students with learning disabilities. Another study showed faster reaction times and subjects reported feeling more energetic after exposure to negative air ions (Tom, Poole, Galla, & Berrier, 1981). Other studies have shown that negative ions introduced into the atmosphere can have a strong impact not only on mood and energy, but on cognitive functioning as well.

⑥ Ionize *This!*

(K–Adult)

Try using an air ionizer to add charged particles to the air. Inexpensive air ionizers can positively affect the mental state of your students. With all this compelling evidence, it seems to be an easy thing to go on the Internet, do a search for air ionizers, and see what comes up. They can be purchased online or in some retail stores as well.

MUSICAL MOMENTS

The power of music in the classroom can be profound and transformational. Research has indicated that music can affect us in ways that can create the conditions for optimal learning. For example, music that affects you emotionally is accompanied by increases in cerebral blood flow to areas of the brain thought to be involved with reward, arousal, motivation, and emotion (Blood & Zatorre, 2001).

Research has indicated numerous positive effects that music has on students. For example, music has been found to facilitate studying, test taking, and learning tasks that require intense concentration (Botwinick, 1997). Studies have shown that using classical or meditative music can produce increased levels of melatonin, a neurotransmitter that plays a key role in relaxation, sleep onset, heart rate, and blood pressure (Tims et al., 1999). Listening to music has been shown to increase spatial reasoning (Rauscher, Shaw, & Ky, 1993) and may even facilitate focused thinking to enhance general intelligence (Cockerton, Moore, & Norman, 1997).

The uses and benefits of using music in the classroom are still being explored, but the message is clear—if you aren't utilizing music in your classroom, you should start.

◎ Music to My Ears

(K–Adult)

There are many ways to use music in your classroom and countless selections and styles to choose from. Don't limit yourself to just playing classical music—use whatever is already in your collection as a start. Notice how listening to a certain piece of music makes you feel, and play it when you want your students to feel the same way. Use music for a purpose and then shut it off! If you have music playing in the background during the entire day, the students will eventually tune it out, and the power of the music to affect the state of the class is lost. Use music for an exact purpose, such as those listed below:

+ To excite students and generate a lot of positive energy, play up-tempo, upbeat music. Anthologies and collections of golden oldies have a broad appeal.
+ If you want to set a quiet and contemplative tone as students enter your room or during a transition, play slow-tempo classical music or music by modern composers such as Gary Lamb.
+ Using music as a trigger to automate daily classroom rituals and routines can be extremely powerful, motivating, and effective. For example, instead of telling students it's time to put away their books for lunch or clean up their workstations after a lesson, use music to prompt the transition. With practice, students will automatically put their work away, get their lunch boxes, and line up at the door when they hear the cue song. Musical cues are fun for students and help reduce stress on the teacher—at the very least you won't have to raise your voice to be heard above the noise of a class working on projects.
+ Match musical routines to songs with appropriate lyrics. Alert your class that it's lunchtime with songs such as

"Be Our Guest" from the Disney movie *Beauty and the Beast*, or "Hot Lunch Jam" from the *Fame* soundtrack.

✦ Use songs such as "Come on Over" by Shania Twain to accompany students as they move around the room.

✦ At the end of the day, send your group home to "So Long, Farewell" from *The Sound of Music,* or "Who Let the Dogs Out" by the Baha Men.

✦ Greet students as they enter your room each morning with an upbeat song to get them in the mood to learn and have fun.

✦ Music can also be used to "entrain" information into the brain. For example, putting academic content to music can be a very effective technique for getting students to memorize information. Try having students write lyrics to familiar songs, such as "Mary Had a Little Lamb" or "Twinkle, Twinkle Little Star," based on the lesson being studied.

VARYING YOUR INSTRUCTION

Psychologist William James (1980) suggested that we have two basic types of attention: voluntary attention and involuntary attention. Voluntary attention requires the brain to actively block out competing stimuli in the environment. Prolonged periods of voluntary attention tend to fatigue the brain's neural inhibitory mechanisms (located in the frontal lobe region), thus enabling competing stimuli to sneak into the brain's awareness. According to James, to keep students' attention, teachers must continually find ways to vary the presentation of the topic to keep it fresh for the students.

If you find yourself lecturing more than you would like, try these activities to spice up your teaching style.

⑤ Change the Visual Field

(K–Adult)

One element you can instantly change (thereby keeping attention) is the students' visual field. Changing your body posture or behavior can be quite unexpected yet very easily accomplished.

+ If you usually stand up to teach, sit down, stand on a chair, or lie on the floor.
+ Before you tell a story or introduce a new topic, turn your back to the audience for a few seconds to capture their interest.
+ Host a guest speaker.
+ Try showing video clips or a computer slide show during your presentation.
+ Go on a field trip.

⑨ Actively Involve the Students

(K–Adult)

Research on enriched environments reveals that active involvement is required to grow connections in the brain. It is not enough to just sit and simply watch events happen (Diamond, 1988). In a study of the impact of enriched environments on dendritic growth, a group of rats lived in an environment with lots of toys, novelty, stimulation, and rat companions. These rats exhibited a great deal of dendritic growth. Rats kept by themselves in cages devoid of any stimulation save the ability to observe the rats in the enriched environments showed no dendritic growth. The importance of this discovery is clear: to grow new connections in their brains, students must interact with their environment and one another. Try incorporating some of the ideas listed below:

+ Recruit a student to teach part of the lesson, or assign an entire lesson to a small group.
+ Have students write and perform skits, role play, tutor each other, or work together on projects. The more you can actively involve students, the better.
+ Add variety when asking for responses from the class. For example, instead of asking students to raise their

hands if they agree with a statement, have them stand up or sit down, move to one side of the room or another, and so on.

✦ Try having students rank order topics in order of importance. For example, ask them, "In order of importance, discuss in your groups and list the most pressing problem in the world today: poverty, hunger, or war." This activity has always generated a great deal of student discussion and involvement for me!

❂ Tell a Story/Use a Metaphor

(K–Adult)

Humans are natural storytellers. For untold generations, the oral history of the species was handed down through stories. Complex ideas have been understood and explained orally through metaphors and storytelling

Humans have an incredible capacity for remembering visual information. Vivid and descriptive storytelling can have a positive cognitive and emotional effect on learning (Sturm, 1999). Until students can picture in their minds what you are teaching them, they will not truly comprehend the concept. To aid memory and comprehension, wise educators experiment with stories and metaphors in their teaching, often having students create their own. Research supports the fact that imagery and emotional response are central to reading and literacy comprehension (Goetz & Sadoski, 1996).

When a state change is needed, telling a story that ties into the subject, or sharing a metaphor that helps students understand the material being taught are highly effective techniques.

✦ Personal stories are wonderful. If you need inspiration, read books like *Chicken Soup for the Soul* (Canfield & Hansen, 1993), or subscribe to magazines like *Bits and Pieces* (Ragan Communications) that have monthly installments of stories, anecdotes, jokes, and quotations.

NOVELTY AND SURPRISE

Surprise and novelty can activate emotional and attentional mechanisms in the brain to enhance learning. One way researchers have examined the role of emotions is by showing college students two sets of film clips—one with emotionally charged content and one with relatively neutral content. When asked to recall details of the film clips two weeks later, the students recalled significantly more about the emotional films than the neutral films (Guy & Cahill, 1999).

That being said, there is a caution: classrooms must contain a balance of novelty and ritual.

Too much novelty and not enough ritual can lead to chaos. But too much ritual and not enough novelty may lead to boredom. We love surprises! When exposed to unexpected rewards, the nucleus accumbens, an area considered the pleasure center of the brain, shows increased activity (Berns, Cohen, & Mintun, 1997). Such research seems to suggest that the element of surprise makes an experience more rewarding to the brain—triggering an emotional response and therefore making it more likely to be remembered.

The message seems clear—incorporating novelty and surprise into the learning environment is a good idea.

The point of the following state changes is to have fun by deliberately doing something you ordinarily wouldn't do. What is the worst that could happen? Even if you feel silly, you will look confident and your audience will welcome the change.

⑥ Stand Still

(K–Adult)

Standing perfectly still while teaching is actually quite unnatural and will be noticed very quickly.

◎ Props

(K–Adult)

✦ Wear a costume to introduce a historical character or a specific period in history.
✦ Use props, magic tricks, or unusual objects to spice up a lesson.

◎ Sound Effects

(K–Adult)

Accentuate your lesson with sound effects. Over the years, I have collected or made several inexpensive mechanisms to create sound effects. I have a tube with a spring that makes a sound like thunder that I purchased at a science museum store. I have a birdcall on a string that I picked up at a nature center. I love having it around my neck and telling students to discuss a topic until they hear the bird sing! After the appropriate interval, I use the birdcall and watch their faces light up with surprise.

✦ When you put a new overhead transparency on the projector, have students tap a drum roll on their desk, followed by them imitating a cymbal crash by clapping their hands together when you turn on the projector lamp.

◎ Keep Them Guessing!

(K–Adult)

✦ Entice your students with a mystery bag with some hidden object in it that they must guess, or present them with a puzzle to solve. Perhaps hide something in the room for participants to find that has something to do with your lesson.

✦ Conclude lessons and classes with "cliff-hanger" questions. For example, tell your students, "One of the greatest mysteries of mankind was found in a period almost a century ago. That mystery is . . . the first topic we will discuss tomorrow morning." This will keep the students guessing and increase interest and anticipation for the next day!

⊚ Passing Out Resources

(K–Adult)

Passing out resources, such as handouts, is an often-overlooked source of excellent state changes that are novel, exciting, and fun.

✦ Throw papers over the heads of students, letting the papers drift down so students have to pick them up, instead of passing them out one by one.

✦ Hide your course syllabus or homework assignment somewhere in the room and have students locate it.

✦ Have student volunteers pass out papers. Before students receive their copy, they each must compliment the person who is distributing the handout.

✦ As a review, each student must recite a fact from the previous lesson before they receive a copy of the resource.

✦ Before students receive their copy of your papers, they must first tell you their name, and then they must introduce you to the person sitting behind them. For example, "Hi, my name is Bob, and I would like to introduce you to Beatrice."

✦ Require students to tell the class a joke before they get their copy of the papers (set in advance the parameters for acceptable humor). Keep a few joke books handy for students to peruse during a break so no one is caught unprepared.

✦ Give the setup of a joke to some students and its punch line to others (you will need more than one joke for this variation). When they find each other, they introduce themselves and tell the joke to the class before you give them their copies of the papers.

☺ Jenga Review
(Grade 3–Adult)

There is a game in which rectangular sticks are stacked in layers to create a tower. I purchased several of these games, and wrote review questions on each stick. Each time someone pulls a stick, they must answer the review question written on the stick. A friend of mine came up with a better idea. She gives the students a sheet with a numbered list of review questions on it, and puts the numbers on the sticks. The students must answer the review question on their sheet that corresponds to the number on the stick.

Playing classroom versions of *Jeopardy* or bingo are also fun ways to review for a test.

☺ Accent on Success!
(Grade 3–Adult)

The teacher speaks with a different accent for an entire day or for a predetermined length of time, like until lunch, for half an hour, until the test is over, and so on. Sample accents could include French, Arnold Schwarzenegger, valley girl, Southern, Texas, British, pirate voice, or a cartoon voice that sounds like Donald Duck, Mickey Mouse, or some other character.

- ✦ Have students also talk in accents for a few minutes. Make sure to model a variety of accents so the students realize they already have several dialects in their heads.
- ✦ If speaking with an accent is too risky for your group, try having them use a different accent only when asking a question.
- ✦ If that is still too risky, have them ask questions in their normal voice, but they must end it with either:
  - A pirate Rrrr, as in, "Did you say Columbus had three ships . . . Rrrrr?"

- A Northern "eh?" as in, "So, A flat and G sharp are the same note . . . eh?

Or use other variations that you come up with, of course being sensitive at all times to all cultural issues so as not to offend.

◎ Theme Days

(Grade 3–Adult)

The first step in instruction, according to the model espoused by noted educator Robert Gagné (1985), is to use what he termed an "interest device" to gain the students' attention.

The first step to getting information into long-term memory is to open up the perceptual register and make sure the information gets into the brain in the first place. Having novel and enjoyable activities such as the theme days listed below can make the classroom atmosphere fun, and can be great "interest devices" to get the kids' attention. Have fun!

Bruce and Sheila Day

Have a Bruce and Sheila day. All the boys are named Bruce, all the girls are named Sheila, and are addressed that way for the day. Add a few "g'day mates" in there for good measure.

Pirate Day

Have a pirate day during which everyone speaks like a pirate—start if off with a few pirate jokes:

- ✦ Rrrrr! Why didn't the pirate like the movie? It was rated Rrrrr.
- ✦ What's a pirate's favorite restaurant? Arrrr-by's.
- ✦ What's a pirate's favorite clothing designer? Arrr-mani.

Jamaican Day

Have a Jamaican day by saying "mon" after every sentence—like, "Thanks for your question, mon," or "Jimmy, please pass out these papers, mon."

How You Doin'? Day

Use the phrase, "How *you* doin'?" every time you speak, as in, "Would you please turn to page 137 and ask it 'How *you* doin'?"

The Left Is Right-On Day

Do everything left-handed for a day. If some students are left-handed, either ask them to change, or have them stay left-handed and enjoy.

Speak Differently Day

Try various ways to speak, such as the ones listed below. Doing this is great fun, but pace yourself—you may want to try it for an hour, but not the entire day.

+ Talk with an echo day, ay ay ay.
+ Slow down and speed up while you're talking day.
+ Every other word is loud day.
+ Talk like a robot day.
+ Talk as fast as you can day.
+ Announce the punctuation day: "Wow, comma that sounds great exclamation point."

◎ To Get Volunteers

(Grade 3–Adult)

Choosing groups or teams in random and unexpected ways enhances team spirit and encourages better interaction among group members because of the feelings of equality it engenders (Klein & Kim, 1998; Miles & Klein, 1998).

✦ Choosing a volunteer to begin an activity can also be an occasion for a surprise. Have students number off from one to five, but (surprise) choose number three to go first. Or, ask partners to choose who will be "A" and who will be "B," then choose "B" first.

✦ Designate roles rather than sequential numbers or letters for students to take within small groups. One will be the bathtub, one will be the shower, choose one person to be the sunshine, another to be the rainbow, and so on.

✦ Find the person wearing the most blue then call on the person to his or her right, or start with the person wearing the most jewelry, with the longest hair, or with the biggest watch.

✦ Play a ball-tossing game to music. When the music stops, the person holding the ball answers a question.

VISUAL CONTEXT

Visual context is one of the brain's most powerful memory aides. Changing something's location not only introduces novelty and curiosity but also helps the brain remember it later. If someone asked you what you ate for dinner last Tuesday, you may have trouble remembering until she reminded you of the restaurant you visited. The brain more readily focuses on location than it does on other memory cues like color, hue, shape, or motion (Ackerman, 1992).

Changing location—either where the teacher and class are located during a teaching episode, or changing the seating of the students—can be a great state change, and is in line with our strongly contextual memory.

Group seating arrangements can foster important social and peer interactions among students, although traditional seating is more effective for some activities, like concentrated independent learning. Students who switched from group seating to rows or pairs improved their on-task time with gains of over 30 percent being reported (Hastings & Wood, 2002). But if collaboration, teamwork and problem solving, or community building is the desired outcome of a lesson, group seating is recommended. The point is to be flexible in seating, to be able to adjust to have the ideal seating for the academic task at hand.

◉ Teaching Location
(K–Adult)

As the instructor, have fun and change the location of you or your class every once in a while.

+ Teach your subject in another room.
+ Switch rooms with another teacher for an hour or part of a lesson.
+ Swap classes (and subjects!) with another teacher, even for just a short while.
+ Take your students outside or into the hallway for part of a lesson.
+ Change where you display class notes, overhead slides, or movies. Can you project onto the ceiling or another wall? Ask for a moveable chalkboard or white board and move it to different locations within the room.

◉ Seating
(K–Adult)

Change the perceived front of the room by teaching from the back of the room (or another location) or by moving the chairs and desks to face in a different direction.

◉ Seat Change
(K–Adult)

Since our memory is so contextual, having students change seats can be an excellent state change, as well as helping long-term memory.

+ Give students until the count of 10 to gather their books and find a new seat within their row. Then later on, give them another count of 10 to find a seat in the same position, but in a different row.
+ Have students balance a piece of notebook paper flat on their palm, and move as quickly as they can to a new seat without dropping the paper.
+ Play musical chairs. Have students walk around the room or up and down the aisles, until the music stops. Students take the nearest seat and you continue the lesson.
+ Walk quickly to new seats while holding breath—students can't exhale until they are in their new seats.
+ You could also divide the room into four imaginary quadrants and have students sit in a new quadrant each time they come into the classroom.
+ Give students a list of actions to perform before taking a seat. For example, say, "Touch three things that are blue and then sit in the nearest seat." "Shake hands with five classmates and then find a place to sit on the opposite side of the room." Or, perhaps try working some of the current lesson into this state change, for example, "Before sitting down, touch one natural object and one man-made object." Or, "On your way back to your seat, shake hands with one *señor* and one *señorita*."

⑤ Seating Arrangement

(K–Adult)

+ Experiment with how you arrange student seats. Try using only chairs, tables instead of desks, desks in pods or rows, or a U-shaped configuration.
+ Have students sit in unusual ways, for example, crossing their arms with their non-dominant arm on top, clasping a thumb, or crossing one ankle over the other.
+ For some lessons, invite your students to sit on the floor, on top of their desks, or lie on their stomachs.

PART 2

Get Your
Students' Attention

Getting the attention of your students is of paramount importance to good teaching. Many of the ideas in this section are based on the notion that many of today's students do not have the auditory channel as their preferred learning modality. Yet in classrooms, I often observe teachers trying to capture their students' attention with auditory cues: "Class, may I have your attention please?" "Ladies and gentlemen, your attention up here please," and so on.

This may not be the most effective way to get our students' attention if auditory is not their preferred learning modality. In fact, I believe that most of our students are visual or kinesthetic in their learning modality preference. In this section are many ways to get students involved and to get their attention using visual or kinesthetic activities.

STATE OF THE CLASS

As an instructor, I am by nature energetic and excited. I sometimes forget that my students may not be as excited as I am, or that they may have other things on their minds they have to deal with before they can focus on the lesson at hand. To be optimally effective as an instructor, I need to find ways to determine what the emotional state of the class is, and to facilitate that state to be as positive as possible. Indeed, Ledoux (1996) has shown us that the systems of emotions and meaning are so interconnected that chemicals of emotions are released virtually simultaneously with cognition. Feelings matter!

Other researchers (for example, Anders & Berg, 2005) have shown evidence that positive attitude change was associated with more motivated behavior on the part of the students, while a negative change was linked to less motivated behavior. Students with positive attitude changes exhibit fewer negative views of educational factors, which means less downshifting, more of a chance to get the input put in, and a greater chance that the curriculum can get transferred to long-term memory.

The following activities can be useful to promote state change, can give the teacher invaluable feedback about the emotional state of the students, and can be a powerful acknowledgement of the students' thoughts, feelings, and emotions.

⊚ One-Word Whip

(Grade 4–Adult)

This could be used as a quick check for teachers to see how motivated or distracted the class is during a lesson, or it could be used as a coming-in ritual to give teachers some feedback on each student's frame of mind as they greet each student at the door in the morning.

The one-word whip is just that: students get a chance to say one word that describes how they're feeling at that moment. I get words ranging from excited and amazing to tired and overwhelmed. I sometimes like to do a one-word whip before a state change, then another one afterwards to help judge if the percentage of positive words has increased, telling me the class is more ready to learn.

◉ Weather Report

(Grade 3–Adult)

For the weather report, students are asked to describe or predict the weather inside their heads. Is it sunny and warm, or slightly cloudy, or is there a thunderstorm going on in their head, or a chance of storms later in the day?

◉ Fist to Five

(Grade 3–Adult)

This is an old facilitation technique that I have adapted for this use. The students are asked to think of how they are feeling at a given moment on a scale from zero to five, five being outstanding, energetic, ready to go; three, just going through the motions; one or zero, meaning I have too much on my mind to concentrate on anything right now. When requested by the teacher, the students hold up the appropriate number of fingers—a closed fist represents zero.

FEEDBACK

It has been said that repetition is the mother of learning. Indeed, depending on the difficulty of the material, students' pre-exposure to the material, students' attitudes toward learning, and a host of other factors, students may need to review material many times before the information is transferred into long-term memory. Finding novel and even fun ways to review can be a challenge for the teacher, but exciting and beneficial for the student.

Students should receive some kind of feedback several times an hour. Making students wait days or even weeks until tests and papers are returned to them for feedback about their success is not an optimal brain-compatible technique. Students learn best in an enriched environment. One of the major components of an enriched environment for human beings is immediate feedback on performance (Woodcock & Richardson, 2000).

Neural pathways for new learning are solidified quickly; wrong information can be hardwired just as easily in the brain as correct information and can be difficult to unlearn. Regular feedback can prevent having to undo incorrect learning as well as providing for a fun, effective state change.

Additionally, knowing how we are performing can reduce anxiety and help to avoid downshifting. Downshifting is a biological response of the brain to fear of a real or perceived threat (Hart, 2002). Feedback from the teacher is invaluable, and feedback from peers may be even more motivating and useful in getting lasting results (Druckman & Sweets, 1988).

⊚ Check With Your Neighbor

(Grade 1–Adult)

To facilitate feedback from peers, the teacher may want to have students pair up and have them ask some or all of the following:

+ What is one question you still have about this topic?
+ What is one thing you still want to know?
+ Tell me one thing you have learned about this topic.

⊚ Menu Review

(Grade 3–Adult)

After a break, such as a weekend or vacation, I sometimes start class with a review session.

1. I write one possible topic for review on each of several take-out menus from restaurants.

2. I tell the students I will leave the room, and when I am gone, I instruct them to choose one of the topics to be reviewed written on one of the menus.

3. I leave the class while the students pick the menu upon which their chosen review topic is written.

4. When I come back in, I pretend that I am picking up their mental energy, and can tell which topic they have chosen. With a bit of dramatic flair, I wave my hands over each menu, until I "magically" pick the one they chose. I am always successful in guessing their choice, because I have a secret accomplice in the class. I set it up ahead of time that when I put my hands over the correct menu, my accomplice signals me with a gesture, like pushing her hair out of her eyes, or crossing his hands. I see this out of the corner of my eye, and with a flourish, reveal the menu the class chose while I was out of the room. The students then review that topic as a group.

The menu review is a surefire way to have fun, increase students' positive states, and facilitate an excellent review.

⑤ Even More Ideas

(Grade 4–Adult)

✦ Students rewrite what was just taught into language easy enough for a 10-year-old, or a 5-year-old, to understand.

✦ Students have a future party and act as if they have known some piece of information for decades. For example, if third-grade students have just learned about the three branches of the United States government, perhaps they would have a future party featuring conversations about how they were so excited by the information they learned in third grade that they decided to become a U.S. senator, and describe the process of how a recent bill they wrote became a law.

✦ Ask the class to pretend they are from the past, 20, 30, 40, or even 100 years ago. Then ask them to react to the information that was just taught as if they were living in that previous era.

+ Have students create a graphic organizer (such as a mind map) of what they have just learned. Alternately, they could start a graphic organizer and give it to a partner to complete or add details to.
+ Students pick a partner and re-teach class material that was just presented.
+ With a partner, students share what they think the three most important points of the lesson were.
+ In small groups and to music, students toss a ball randomly around a circle. When the music stops, the teacher asks a question. The person holding the ball must answer it for the group, and the group congratulates her if she is correct, or helps her to come up with the correct answer.
+ Play a short piece of music, perhaps the theme song from the *Jeopardy* game show. Before the music ends, students must write either a question they have about the lesson or a challenging question-and-answer pair that they will read to try to stump the class.

BREATHING

The brain needs oxygen to survive. Although the average brain weighs only about three pounds, it uses about 20 percent of the body's oxygen (Erecinska & Silver, 2001).

Because the brain does not store oxygen, it needs a constant supply of richly oxygenated blood to bring oxygen to the brain. Human beings are designed to get all the oxygen they need from regular physical activity. In schools, kids get great stimulation and lots of oxygen when they are at recess and at play. The challenge comes in when recess times get reduced or eliminated due to budget cuts, or when students are in the classroom for long periods of time. The activities in this section may help ameliorate these circumstances.

As important as oxygen is, research suggests that factors such as mental stress and anxiety can actually rob the brain and body of adequate oxygen by interrupting normal breathing patterns (Bernardi et al., 2000). Deep breaths help to deliver oxygen to the blood for the brain to use to keep fully alert and functionally optimal.

The benefits of proper deep breathing are numerous. For students in school, it can bring rich, oxygenated blood to their brains to help them focus and pay attention. If made a regular part of the school day, deep breathing could even become a lifelong habit with numerous health benefits. For example, medical researchers (Grossman, Grossman, Schein, Zimlichman, & Gavish, 2001) did a study with patients suffering from high blood pressure. The subjects all succeeded in lowering their blood pressure without medication by routinely applied sessions of slow and regular breathing for 10 minutes a day. Studies also indicate that proper breathing exercises can enhance oxygen flow, which can have the effect of reducing heart rate and anxiety (Bernardi et al., 2000).

Most deep breathing should be done through the nose, for several reasons. Our breathing was designed to take place mainly through our nose. When we breathe through our nose, the hairs that line our nostrils filter out particles of dust and dirt that can be injurious to our lungs. If too many particles accumulate on the membranes of the nose, we automatically secrete mucus to trap them or sneeze to expel them.

Another reason to breath through our noses is to maintain the correct balance of oxygen and carbon dioxide in our blood. Research (Weitzberg & Lundberg, 2002) has shown that if we release carbon dioxide too quickly, as we could with mouth breathing, the arteries and vessels carrying blood to our cells constrict and the oxygen in our blood is unable to reach the cells in sufficient quantity. This includes the carotid arteries, which carry blood (and oxygen) to the brain. The lack of sufficient oxygen going to the cells of the brain can actually make our body feel as though it is under attack and begin the "fight or flight" response.

This is all interesting, but if you are a teacher in front of 30 fidgety kids, who cares? Just remember, when possible, have them breathe through their noses.

Activities such as those listed in this section can be great for state changes and can help with students' overall health as well!

Students could do the following state changes at their desks, standing in line, or anytime they need a brain break.

⑥ In One Side, Out the Other

(Grade 3–Adult)

Research (Shannahoff-Khalsa, Boyle, & Buebel, 1991) seems to indicate that we can tell which brain hemisphere is currently dominant by noticing which nostril is currently exhibiting greater airflow. Even more interesting is the finding that cognitive performance can be positively influenced by forcibly altering the breathing pattern by closing up the nostril currently in use and breathing out of the non-dominant nostril.

+ Here's a fun state change that might help students stimulate their non-dominant hemisphere. Have them block off their dominant nostril and take a few deep breaths through their other nostril. Even if no significant cognitive gains are realized, it is funny, funny looking, and fun to do.

⑥ Deep Breathing

(K–Adult)

Have students stop, take several deep breaths through the nose, and exhale slowly through the mouth, or the other way around. The teacher can help facilitate deep, cleansing breaths by counting out loud while students inhale for four counts, followed by a slow exhale for eight counts, then repeat.

⑤ Straw Tongue

(K–Adult)

This looks absolutely silly, and is meant to! Have the students make a straw out of their tongue, and breathe through the straw tongue for one or two breaths. As they exhale, have them try to turn a page or move a paper or pencil across their desk with their laser-like breath. Just remember that not every student is born with the ability to roll his or her tongue, which could lead to an interesting discussion on genetics.

⑤ Breath and Shhh!

(K–Adult)

Have students all take a deep breath, hold it, then let it out in a very intense, karate-like SHHHHHH. Adding hand motions seems to help, like bringing both hands to the chest when breathing in, then pushing hands away from the body on the exhale.

⑤ "Om" School

(K–Adult)

According to researchers in Sweden (Weitzberg, & Lundberg, 2002), humming actually decreases the amount of nitric oxide in sinuses. Amazingly enough, during normal exhalation the amount of nitric oxide exchanged was about 4 percent. When the volunteers hummed, the gas exchange increased to about 98 percent! Because the brain needs a constant supply of richly oxygenated blood flow, increasing the efficiency of the respiratory system through activities such as this could help us pay attention and enjoy optimal brain functioning.

+ Have all students take a deep breath, and as they blow out the breath, ask them to allow their eyes to close (optional) and quietly intone a syllable (om or ahh is recommended).
+ Have a contest in the class to see who can hum or hold the longest on one breath. If you are in a large group,

have students raise their hands if they are still going, and drop them when they are out, or have students stand, then sit when they are out of breath.

⊚ Breathing Ritual

(K–Adult)

Since breathing is so essential to life, try making breathing a part of your classroom routine. Deep, conscious breathing can get more oxygen into the blood. Making deep breathing a part of your classroom rituals can help bring a sense of predictability to students' lives that is so important for their mental well-being.

+ When students are reading aloud in class, have them routinely breathe in at the end of each page, then exhale as they turn to the next page in the book.
+ Use a deep breathing routine to help transitions between activities. For example, when students complete a standing activity, have them take a deep breath, then blow it out, take another deep breath, and as they blow it out, sit down.
+ You could expand upon the fun of this by having the class sit down with different styles of music playing. For example, you might say, "Take a deep breath, let it out, take another deep breath, and as you blow it out, sit down salsa style." When you say "salsa style," begin to play some salsa music. This may sound a bit complicated, but it is really fun, funny, effective, and very easy once you try it. I have had students sit down salsa style, funky style (to the tune of "Brick House"), riverdance style (to the Riverdance soundtrack), seventies disco style (to "Stayin' Alive"), and so on.

Positive rituals and routines such as the breathing activities described above can be excellent ways to give students some predictability in their lives, with the result of calming them down and making them more able to access those parts of their brains they need for school.

HANDS AND ARMS

☺ Hand Fidgets

(K–Adult)

Some students may need more stimulation, some students less stimulation. Hand and mouth fidgets allow students with diverse kinesthetic needs to control and choose the amount and quality of stimulation they receive. Even some adults doodle while on the telephone or jingle change in their pockets while having a conversation. The option to choose the amount and type of stimulation they need empowers students; exercising the freedom to take control of their learning environment can have a profoundly positive effect on their enthusiasm and interest in learning.

The cerebellum, which means "little brain" in Latin, is emerging as being important in many kinds of learning, in particular, spatial ability, which is so important in many school tasks such as mathematics (Leggio et al., 2000). Since motor programs are stored in the cerebellum, the following state changes may help to stimulate the cerebellum and aid in learning.

Provide students with hand and mouth fidgets for an effective kinesthetic state change:

+ Hand fidgets are small items with interesting textures, like finger puppets, Koosh balls, gel-filled balls, or worry stones, that can be manipulated quietly by the student at her desk. Ideally, students are allowed to get a fidget if they feel the need for one. You could make the fidgets available in a box or bag in some area of the room.

+ Mouth fidgets are food items with different tastes and textures that students enjoy. If your environment allows for it, gum chewing is one example of a mouth

fidget. Gum chewing is good as a heavy job for the proprioceptive sensors in your jaw.
+ Introduce snacks with different tastes (salty, sweet, etc.) and textures (smooth, crunchy, etc.) for a kinesthetic state change that will satisfy the need for oral stimulation that some of your students may have.

⑤ There's the Rub!

(K–Adult)

For a quick state change that can provide tactile and proprioceptive input, along with repetitive movement of gross-motor muscles, try having all students rub their hands together super fast for a count of 10.

+ Have students rub their knuckles together, or do a 10-count drumroll on the table.

⑤ Clap On, Clap Off

(Grade 4–Adult)

In this activity, the teacher claps a number of times as quickly as possible, then challenges the students to echo that exact number, at that same speed. The goal is to get everyone in the class to stop at exactly the same time.

+ For example, the teacher could clap exactly nine times, with the class echoing immediately afterwards.
+ Or the teacher and class can clap together.

This fast-paced activity will be sure to get and keep the students' attention, as well as get in some repetitive movements of those important gross-motor muscles. The focus you will get from your students will be amazing—the more competitive they are, the more it seems they will pay attention and love this activity.

◎ The Magic Number Seven

(Grade 4–Adult)

The teacher begins by clapping a seven-count pattern, which the class immediately echoes. Three such seven-count patterns are listed below. Try one at a time with a class, and then try to put all three together one after another with no pauses. Feel free to make up your own patterns.

Pattern one: clap seven times rapidly

Pattern two: lap clap lap clap lap clap lap

Pattern three: lap clap snap clap lap clap snap

◎ Cross Clap

(Grade 3–Adult)

For this state change, the teacher holds his hands far apart vertically, one above the head, one below the waist. The students are instructed to clap whenever the instructor's hands cross each other. The teacher moves his hands up and down several times while students clap; and, of course, there is the inevitable fake out when the teacher begins to move his hands, and then stops.

◎ If You Can Hear Me . . .

(K–Grade 6)

This is a classic teacher move, in which the teacher says, "If you can hear me, clap once" (waits for a response), "If you can hear me clap twice," and so forth.

+ The fun thing about this state change for me is adding novelty, which has a host of positive effects in the classroom. This state change is a great way to get the students' attention, while at the same time adding routine and novelty. The routine comes in if the teacher consistently uses variations of this to get students' attention. The novelty comes from the infinite variations on this theme that creative teachers have shown to me. Try having fun with it, for example, "If you can hear me, clap twice and make this sound (raspberry)," "If you can hear me, put one hand on your head, and the other on your knee," and so on.

VOICE

Novelty drives this state change category as well. People are hardwired to look for and react to novelty and surprise. The brain is particularly responsive to unexpected situations during cognitive tasks (Berns et al., 1997). Use the amazing versatility of the human voice to introduce novel auditory state changes into the classroom. There is an enormous range of possibilities.

⊚ Change Your Voice

(K–Adult)

Change different aspects of your voice, such as:

+ Tempo (how fast you speak)
+ Volume
+ Timbre (vocal quality like nasal or falsetto)
+ Pitch (speaking in a deep or high voice)
+ Celebrity impressions get noticed—even silly, imperfect ones!
+ Read with passion, really hamming it up for emotional impact.
+ Laugh or tell a joke or funny story. Sing or whistle while teaching. When was the last time you did either? Try it!
+ Emphasize important words, phrases, or new or unusual vocabulary by slightly pausing before and after you say them, or else by speaking slowly or changing the quality of your voice for the moment. Writers use bold or italic typeface to make a point, and

to set off new or unusual vocabulary—do the same thing with your voice.

☉ Positive Affirmations

(K–Adult)

In a classroom, most of the positive affirmations of the "good job" and "keep up the good work" variety are passed only from the teacher to the student. But imagine a classroom in which the teacher *and* the students both deliver positive affirmations on a regular basis. This kind of supportive environment can affect students very positively and powerfully.

Affirmations are a wonderful way to facilitate creating a supportive environment in a classroom. Like many of the activities in this book, they help create an atmosphere of mutual trust and support to counteract the student impulse to downshift.

Students who have downshifted have difficulty focusing on anything not directly related to their survival. Positive affirmations can help make students feel good not only for receiving praise but for the chance to interact with others in a warm, friendly way.

✦ A good place to start is at the end of a group or partner exercise. Simply tell the students to turn to their partners and say something positive. Some common affirmations are, "Turn to your partner, give them a high five, and say, 'Great ideas!'" or "Turn to your partner, shake his hand, and say, 'You're a genius!'" and so on.

✦ When having students give each other affirmations, make sure to give them both the words to say, and a motion to go along with the words each time. The addition of a physical action may make an affirmation easier for reluctant students to participate.

✦ Tell students to be creative and come up with new gestures to use. Have them invent gestures on the spot or lead a short brainstorming session for ideas that everyone can use.

⑤ Count Down

(K–Grade 6)

For a quick state change, to refocus the class, or even a fun way to go to a break ("Your group can go to break as soon as you do this task"), try this state change. Everyone in class counts down from five out loud, or counts up from one, at the same time.

✦ Do it with different voices such as a high squeaky falsetto or a low bass.

✦ Count from one to five starting with a very low voice at one, and proceeding to a very high voice by five.

✦ Count from one to five as fast as you can, as slow as you can, as if you were underwater, and so forth.

✦ As a group, say the alphabet backwards as quickly as possible.

✦ Before you go to break, name at least 10 candy bars, or cartoon characters, models of cars, animated movies, and so on.

⑤ Callbacks

(K–Adult)

A callback is when the teacher asks for a specific response from the class.

✦ Callbacks can be used as a way to emphasize important vocabulary (The teacher might say "The process for creating new neurons is called neurogenesis—Is called what?" Class responds "neurogenesis."), and to ensure everyone hears the same message ("We'll take a 10-minute break—How many minutes? Class responds '10.'").

✦ Callbacks can also be used to prime the brain that important information is coming up. We are more likely to see something and pay attention to information if we are told to look for it.

Therefore, try priming the brains of your students to see the good in their classmates by using positive callbacks. For example, "If you can hear me, say 'uh huh,'" "If you think you're awesome say 'I'm awesome,'" "If you think you're partner's awesome, say 'I knew that . . .'"

✦ To help reduce threat by making your rituals and routines predictable, try making callbacks part of your classroom routine by using them consistently as part of your facilitation and teaching.

⑥ Look This Way!

(Grade 3–Adult)

This is a very quick, and very effective way to get kids' attention focused on you. The success of this activity depends on the instructors' enthusiasm and energy, so be excited when you point up at the ceiling and say loudly to the kids, "Look at the ceiling." Then almost immediately and in rapid-fire progression, "Look over there (to the left)," "Look that way (to the right)," "Look at me!" Then immediately start talking about your topic.

CROSS LATERALS

The brain is divided into two hemispheres and connected by a band of fibers called the corpus callosum. Anything that crosses the vertical midline of our bodies visually or kinesthetically is good for our brain, encourages communication between the hemispheres, and stimulates our attentional systems.

Almost 55 percent of students in the third and fifth grades who participated in cross-lateral activities for 15 minutes a day were known to improve their reading scores on standardized tests (Koester, 2001).

Crossing the midline with activities such as the ones in this section has been shown to affect the performance of fine-motor skills (Smits-Engelsman, Van Galen, & Michelis, 1995).

Students who were involved in cross-lateral activities were more accurate in motor activities such as writing and pointing. Therefore, these can be not only great state changes, but may help develop some skills in the students and increase the activity between the hemispheres of their brains. Some of these activities are adapted from *The Brain Gym* (Dennison, 1989), which is a great resource for more cross-lateral activities.

⊚ Nose/Ear Switch

(Grade 3–Adult)

1. With your left hand, grab your nose.

2. With your right hand, cross over your left hand and grab your left ear.

3. Switch, so that your right hand is now grabbing your nose, and your left hand is crossed over the right and grabbing your right ear.

4. Repeat several times.

5. Try it standing up.
   - See which students can do it the fastest.
   - Do it in rhythm with music.
   - Add a clap in between the switches.

⊚ Finger/Thumb Switch

(Grade 3–Adult)

1. On one hand, hold up your index finger.

2. On your other hand, hold up your thumb.

3. Simultaneously switch as fast as you can, so that whichever hand held up the index finger up now has the thumb up, and the hand that had the thumb up now has the index finger up.

4. Repeat several times.

- Try it standing up.
- See which students can switch their fingers and thumbs the fastest.

⑥ Hook-Ups

(K–Adult)

1. Stand up.

2. Stand up and extend your arms out in front of you, palms facing each other.

3. Bring your palms together until they pass each other and cross at the wrists.

4. With your wrists crossed, turn your palms to face each other and interlock your fingers.

5. Bring your locked hands in toward your body and turn them so they face up.

6. Cross your legs at the knees or ankles.

7. Relax your tongue on the roof of your mouth.

8. Take three or four deep breaths through your nose.

9. Unclasp your hands and shake them out.

⑥ The Hook-Up Game

(Grade 4–Adult)

1. Everyone choose a partner.

2. Decide who will be A, and who will be B.

3. B's "hook up" as described previously.

4. A's point to, without touching, one of B's clasped fingers.

5. B's must wiggle the finger at which the A's are pointing.

6. Repeat with several fingers.

7. Switch: A's hook up, B's point.
   - Try it with the eyes of the hooked-up partner shut. Partners touch the finger they want wiggled.

◎ Cross Crawl

(K–Grade 5)

1. Stand up.

2. Slowly march in place.

3. While marching, touch knee with opposite hand. In other words, when left knee comes up, tap it with the right hand; when right knee comes up, tap it with the left hand.

◎ Slapping Leather

(K–Grade 5)

Same as above, but feet go behind, and each hand slaps the heel of the opposite shoe (left hand reaches behind and slaps right heel, etc.).

◎ Lazy Eights

(K–Grade 5)

1. Stand up.

2. Extend one arm in front of you with the thumb pointing up and the other fingers curled toward the palm. Center the thumb in front of your nose.

3. Holding head still, looking straight ahead, move hand, with thumb extended, in a large, horizontal figure eight, making sure the pattern crosses at the midline of your body.

4. Without moving your head, follow the thumb with your eyes.

5. Repeat several times.
   • Try with alternating hands.
   • Try with one eye shut.

☺ Windshield Wiper

(K–Grade 5)

Instructor puts some music on, such as "Car Wash" by Rose Royce. Ask students to put an elbow in one hand, and pretend to wipe windows to the beat, switching hands with the beat.

☺ Window Washer

(K–Grade 5)

This is best done with a prop that the students can hold in their hands, such as a washcloth (purchased at the local dollar store), a paper towel, or even a sponge. Music is played while the students take their right hand and pretend to wash a window on their left side, and then switch.

☺ Climb the Ladder to Success

(K–Grade 5)

Again, it is best to do this activity to up-tempo music with a strong beat. Students sit or stand at their desks and pantomime climbing a ladder. The teacher can add to the fun by narrating the journey—for example, "Using your right hand, pick an apple way over to your left-hand side," "Oh, here comes a squirrel," "A big breeze is coming, hold on tight and keep climbing," and so forth.

☺ Pat Yourself on the Back

(K–Adult)

Students pat themselves on the back, pat the shoulder on the same side, opposite side, cross arms and pat both sides at once, pat a neighbor's shoulder, and so on.

☺ Itsy Bitsy Spider

(K–Adult)

This is a great twist on a perennial favorite.

1. Students stand up and find a partner.

2. The entire class sings and does the motions to the children's classic "Itsy Bitsy Spider."

3. Partners stand side by side, shoulder to shoulder.

4. All sing "Itsy Bitsy Spider" again, with partners doing the motions together. Partners on the left may only use their left hand, and partners on the right may only use their right hand. They do the motions working their opposite hands together.

☺ Ear You Go!

(K–Adult)

For a fun and perhaps soothing state change, have students hold both of their earlobes and gently massage. For cross-lateral benefit, have them switch sides, and grab their left ear with their right hand, and their right ear with their left hand and gently massage.

Isn't this interesting? The earlobes have been identified as a nexus for nerve stimulation in such diverse fields as acupuncture, reflexology, and auriculotherapy (Oleson, 2002). Activities such as these are novel state changes and could have the added benefits of a bit of therapeutic massage.

HEAVY JOBS

In each of our joints there are *proprioceptive* sensors that help us determine and keep track of the way our body is moving in space. The proprioceptive sense is what allows us to touch our nose when our eyes are shut, for example. If students do not have a well-developed proprioceptive sense, they may display behaviors such as being awkward with their gross-motor movements.

It is my belief that if students have difficulty finding their way around the greater space around them, it is much more difficult for students to find their way around the much more confined space of a written page in a book. To stimulate the proprioceptive sense, occupational therapists suggest doing activities called "Heavy Jobs," or "Heavy Work."

Heavy work activities are considered resistive and stimulate the proprioceptive receptors because they involve elements of push, pull, lift, and carry (Kranowitz, Szklut, Balzer-Martin, Haber, & Sava, 2001). Trying out the following activities can help develop students' proprioceptive sense, and are great state changes besides.

◎ Start the Presses!

(K–Grade 8)

Students stand up, stand behind their chairs, pick up the chair, and hold it. If the space and the maturity of the group allows, students can walk around their desk or table with the chair as well.

◎ Portable Library

(K–Grade 8)

If you have a student who may need more of a state change, have a stack of books in a corner, and ask them to take the stack to the teacher next door or down the hall. This set of books could travel many times during the course of the year. It is suggested that you give tips on the proper way to lift, such as keeping a straight back and lifting with the legs.

◎ Chair-y Baby!

(K–Grade 12)

Have students put their hands on their chairs and do push-ups on their chairs.

⊚ Wall Push-Ups

(K–Grade 12)

Have students stand up, find a space along a wall, and do standing push-ups against the wall.

NOVEL MOVEMENTS

Habitual movements, like walking and chewing gum, are carried out for the most part at the subconscious level. Not so with novel movements. A movement that is novel to our system makes the brain shift focus and pay attention, because it has no memories to rely on for the execution of a novel stimulus. The prefrontal cortex is engaged, along with the rear two-thirds of the frontal lobes. These areas are often used for higher-order thinking skills, such as problem solving, planning, and sequencing new things to learn and do (Calvin, 1996).

There are numerous other benefits to incorporating novel movements. As mentioned previously, the brain needs a constant flow of blood to bring it oxygen and nutrients. Novel events and activities have been found to increase blood flow in several areas of the brain (Tulving, Markowitsch, Craik, Habib, & Houle, 1996).

Novel movements can also help stimulate the brain to be curious about and interested in the task at hand (Berlyne, 1960). Teachers love to spark their students' curiosity, and stimuli that are novel and surprising can have that effect.

The following activities may be novel enough for your students to give them a change of state, and maybe have some of the added benefits mentioned above as well.

⊚ You Want Me To Do *What?*

(Grade 3–Adult)

While sitting at a desk or standing have students move their right foot clockwise while attempting to trace the number six with their right hand in the air.

⑨ What's in a Name?

(Grade 4–Adult)

Have students stand and balance with one foot slightly out in front of them. Tell them to rotate their foot at the ankle in either direction. As they rotate their foot, challenge them to write their name in the air with their elbow. Vary the activity by having them write their name with any body part (perhaps the nose) except the hand, or make the activity more challenging by requiring students to write with one side of the body and rotate the foot on the opposite side.

⑨ Sticky Fingers

(Grade 4–Adult)

✦ Students are asked to place both palms together, and then bend both middle fingers down until the first joints of both middle fingers are touching. Without breaking contact, have them try to separate the remaining fingertips—the fourth fingers will act like they are glued together and won't come apart.

✦ Students can place one hand, palm down on their desk. They are then asked to bend their middle finger until the first joint is touching the table. The teacher then asks them to move each finger in turn, ending with the fourth finger, which, again, won't move as long as the first joint of the middle finger maintains contact with the table.

⑨ Chair Surfing

(Grades 3–8)

While playing the Beach Boys' "Surfin' Safari," or a similar tune, have the students stand on their chairs and pretend they are surfing. If they can't handle chairs, do it on the floor. You can help facilitate some of the fun by giving a running dialogue of their surfing trip—"Here comes a big wave, get ready . . ."

◎ Back-Words Writing

(Grades 3–8)

Students pair up and make a symbol or write a letter or word on their partner's back, and the partner guesses the word.

+ This activity is great for a foreign language vocabulary review.
+ Try using this activity for a game show-like review. Try Reverse *Jeopardy*, where the word is the answer and the partner must guess the question, or have them write it on their partner's back.

◎ *Can* Touch This!

(K–Adult)

As the students go back to their seats after an activity, tell them to touch certain things in the room on the way back to their desks. Examples include touch three blue things, one piece of glass, two pieces of jewelry, two walls, and so on.

◎ Eyebrow Olympics

(K–Grade 5)

Have students move their eyebrows up and down together as fast as they can. You could also have them try to move each eyebrow individually up and down as fast as they can.

+ For something really humorous, have them pretend they are in the eyebrow Olympics, and have them do a fancy eyebrow dismount and stick it. Have them perform this feat for their neighbor and award points if they can make their neighbor laugh.

◎ That Face Rings a Bell!

(Grades 3–8)

A group of students choose a leader to make facial expressions. While the leader makes these expressions, the students try to guess the emotion being portrayed, getting a point for each correct guess. When a team has logged five points, they can go to break. It would be helpful for the teacher to model a range of possibilities for the students before they do this activity by showing them some sample faces and having them practice. Sample expressions could include fear, anxiety, curiosity, conceit, surprise, anger, joy, triumph, amusement, and so forth.

The frontal lobe comes on line slowly, taking years to fully mature. For example, the emotional regulation capability is not fully operational until after adolescence (Sowell, Thompson, Holmes, Jernigan, & Toga, 1999). The ability to read the subtleties of facial expressions is another frontal lobe skill that may not be fully mature in younger students. This state change is fun, and who knows? Maybe it could help develop some of those skills in reading facial expressions so important to human communication.

PART 3

Energize
Your Students

What strategies help energize students in the classroom? Marian Diamond, a pioneer in brain research, recommended involving students in social activities for a *significant* part of instructional activities (Diamond & Hopson, 1998). According to Glasser (1986), children's motivation to work in elementary school is dependent on the extent to which their basic psychological needs are met. Cooperative learning increases student motivation by providing peer support. Cooperative learning promotes academic achievement, is relatively easy to implement, and is not expensive. Children's improved behavior and attendance, and increased enjoyment of school, are some of the benefits of cooperative learning (Slavin, 1987).

Cooperative learning helps students feel successful at every academic level. In cooperative learning teams, low-achieving students can make contributions to a group and experience success, and all students can increase their understanding of ideas by explaining them to others (Featherstone, 1986).

Having a fun classroom and an engaging, humorous instructor makes coming to class enjoyable, and can also increase teaching effectiveness. One study (Adamson, O'Kane, & Shevlin, 2005) showed a direct relation between student perception of how funny the instructor was and the effectiveness of the teaching.

Getting Into Groups

If you are getting kids into groups anyway, why not try to do it in a fun way that will be a state change and maybe elicit laughter, which would then get more oxygen into the bloodstream? The following are just some of the successful methods I have used to get students into groups.

⊚ Barnyard Animals

(K–Adult)

Have students make the sound of their favorite barnyard animal, and keep making that sound until they find all of the people in the room that are making the same sound. You may want to limit it to a few animals, such as cow, dog, chicken, donkey, cat—almost every child should be able to pull off a passable rendition of any of those animals.

✦ With a little prep work, you could facilitate the size of each group by writing animal names on note cards and passing them out—five chicken cards, five cow cards, and so on.

⊚ Rock/Paper/Scissors

(Grade 3–Adult)

Another fun way to get students into groups is to have all students do rock/paper/scissors and find all their partners, that is, all rocks get together, all papers get together, all scissors get together.

⑥ Magnet Groups

(Grade 3–Adult)

I went to the dollar store, oops, I mean, the "teacher store," and bought a bunch of random objects to pass out. Once I got lucky, and you might too, by finding about eight groups of about six different refrigerator magnets or other unusual objects small enough to hold in your hand. I have students grab a magnet during a break, and then they must arrange themselves according to who has matching magnets.

⑥ Ocular Contract

(Grade 4–Adult)

I have students silently look around the room, and using only their eyes and facial expressions, choose their groups or partners before we get up and move to join the partner or group they silently chose.

⑥ Telephone

(Grade 3–Adult)

With students in rows, the teacher whispers a direction into the ear of the first person in each row. They in turn whisper it to the person behind them, and so on until the message travels down the rows to everyone. The message I usually whisper is something like "When I say 'Horton Hears a Who,' stand up and get into your groups." I love the looks of surprise when I say the phrase at the end of the game, and get some confused stares!

RANDOM GROUPINGS

Curiosity, novelty, and surprise used at the beginning of a lesson are known to be effective teaching techniques (Small &

Arnone, 2000). An enriched environment—one in which novelty, surprise, feedback, and social interaction play a significant role—has been found to elicit neuroanatomical and behavioral changes, such as proliferation of dendritic growth; the formation of new glia cells, a process called gliogenesis; and the formation of new neurons, a process known as neurogenesis (Van Praag, Kempermann, & Gage, 1999). Activities such as the ones listed below make the learning environment enjoyable, and may help brain development as well.

⊚ Silent Arrangement

(Grade 4–Adult)

Tell students to arrange themselves in a line by various attributes (some suggestions are listed below), and have them accomplish this feat without talking.

Try having students arrange themselves by

+ Birthday month.
+ Height, tallest to shortest, or shortest to tallest.
+ Alphabetically by first name/last name/middle name.
+ Hair length, longest to shortest, or shortest to longest.
+ Most jewelry on to least jewelry on.
+ Shoe size, largest to smallest, or smallest to largest.
+ Last digit of their home telephone number, zero to nine.
+ The first number of their home address.
+ Where they were born, from closest to the school to farthest away (have them share locations when they are finished).
+ The total number of letters in their full name, from least to most.

⊚ Random Favorites

(Grade 3–Adult)

This could start off as a state change/team-building activity, without the students knowing that the eventual purpose is to get them into groups for an academic purpose. Have students go to different areas of the room as a way of voting with their feet.

✦ Favorite vacation: Would you rather vacation at an amusement park (go to one place in the room), in the mountains (point to another area in the room for the students to go to), or at the beach (show them another area to go to, and give them a few moments to arrange themselves)?
✦ Favorite spectator sport: NASCAR, tennis, or baseball?
✦ Favorite food: Italian food, Mexican food, or hamburgers?
✦ Favorite sports activity: Swimming, skiing, or rollerblading?
✦ Favorite car: Porsche, monster truck, or a junker?

GET STUDENTS UP AND MOVING

There are many benefits to being an active and physically fit child. Active children have fewer cardiovascular risk factors and have lower rates of coronary heart disease (Ross & Pate, 1987). If students have poor muscle tone in their core muscles, such as legs, backs, and abdomen, it may be difficult for them to sit upright in a chair by a desk all day, making it difficult to attend to the lessons at hand. (Could this masquerade as attention deficit hyperactivity disorder [ADHD]?)

There are numerous other benefits of regular exercise. Van Praag, Christie, Sejnowski, and Gage (1999) conducted animal studies that suggest running and other aerobic exercise can activate neurogenesis, which is the growth of new brain cells in certain areas of the brain. Regular exercise such as running can also raise levels of glucose, which is fuel for the brain, along with levels of neurotransmitters such as serotonin, epinephrine, and dopamine that work to inhibit hunger and help regulate moods.

Exercise can also increase blood flow throughout the body, including to the brain. Increased blood flow to the brain can help the brain get the oxygen and nutrients it needs for optimal functioning. Novel activities such as the ones in this section have been shown to be associated with increased cerebral cortical blood volume (Peyton, Bass, Burke, & Frank, 2005) and can have a positive emotional impact on students and help them pay attention.

Lastly, these activities are fun. Every group I have worked with has laughed all the way through them. Data from research (Schmidt, 1994) suggests that material presented in a humorous manner increases attention and recall compared to information presented in a non-humorous fashion. While the state changes listed here are not given as ways to present material, they do represent the power of humor to shape classroom environments, assist in getting the input put in, bond classmates together, and help students recall the information later.

ⓖ Triangle Tag

(Grade 4–Adult)

A large open area, like a gymnasium, or going outside is required for this game. Students separate into groups of four.

1. Three people join hands. They decide who will be "It."

2. The fourth person tries to tag "It" while the other two in the circle move to protect "It."

ⓖ Bodyguard and Secret Agent

(Grade 4–Adult)

1. Each student silently decides which other student in the class will be the secret agent out to get his secrets.

2. Each student also chooses who will be his bodyguard. The goal is for the students to keep the bodyguard between them and the secret agent at all times. The fun is that only the students know who the secret agent is and who their bodyguard is.

3. When the teacher gives the signal, students move around the room, attempting to keep their bodyguard in between them and their secret agent.

⑥ Conduct the Orchestra

(K–Adult)

This is a great kinesthetic state change that really gets kids to move! I play some rousing music, maybe Tchaikovsky's *1812 Overture* or something else equally stirring. I ask students to stand and conduct the imaginary orchestra with different parts of their bodies. For example:

✦ Conduct with your left hand.
✦ Conduct your right hand.
✦ Conduct with both hands.
✦ Conduct with a foot.
✦ Conduct with your head.
✦ Conduct with your head, one foot, and your eyes.

CIRCLE GAMES

Excessive worry over tests, grades, and overall academic achievement can impair both cognition and physical health (Ashcraft & Kirk, 2001). The following games can increase student bonding, thereby helping to lower the sense of the classroom as a threatening place, and improving the environment for learning. Such group activities have also been shown to lead to increased commitment to academic effort and school values (Holloway, 2000).

In addition, scientists have found that there is a positive correlation between the level of body activity and the behavioral state. In other words, gross-motor activities like walking have been found to increase the activity of neurons that produce the neurotransmitter serotonin, which helps to regulate moods (Jacobs & Fornal, 1997). This is yet another piece of evidence that shows a relationship between motor activity and afferent inputs (signals going into the brain) that can positively affect the mental state. The message—get kids up and moving.

Incredibly, research has also indicated that the level of movement ability in students was found to have a positive impact on their perception of their athletic and scholastic competence (Piek, Baynum, & Barrett, 2006). An implication of this research seems to be that students who have more opportunity for more movement could increase their movement ability and enjoy the excellent side benefit of increased self-esteem.

Numerous studies have also indicated that physical activity can have many positive effects, including increased test scores, particularly in the area of mathematics (Shephard, 1997; Shephard et al., 1984). Other benefits that have been linked to physical activity include increased concentration, and improved reading and writing test scores (Symons, Cinelli, James, & Groff, 1997).

⑥ If You're Clappy and You Know It . . .

(Grade 3–Adult)

This is a fun stand-alone activity, or you can utilize it as a ritual to signify the end of a circle activity.

While students are standing in a circle, they put their hands out to their sides, and clap a predetermined number of times with the people on both sides of them. For example, the instructor might say, "OK, everyone must clap 11 times. It sounds like this." Instructor claps very quickly 11 times, and then invites the class to follow.

⑥ Circle Sit

(Grade 5–Adult)

1. Have the entire group of students stand in a tight circle, shoulder to shoulder, facing the center.

2. Direct the students to make a quarter turn to the right, so that they face the back of their neighbor's head and their left shoulders are inside the circle.

3. Now have everyone gently place both of their hands on the shoulders of the person in front of them.

4. Walk around the circle, encouraging them to make it as tight as possible—they'll need to be very close for the next step.

5. Finally, instruct the students to slowly sit down on the knees of the person behind them. If the circle seems stable and confident, encourage them to slowly lift their hands in the air and cheer!

6. Dismantle the circle by having students put their hands back on the shoulders of the person in front of them and waiting for your cue so they all stand at once.
   • You can also make this circle in the opposite direction.

☺ Gotcha!

(Grade 4–Adult)

1. Tell all students to stand in a tight circle, shoulder to shoulder.

2. Have the students put their left hand, palm facing up, in front of the person to their left.

3. Next, the students should extend the index finger on their right hand and place it in the palm of the person on their right (whose upturned palm is in front of them).

4. When the instructor says "Go," students try to do two things simultaneously: lift their right finger out of their neighbor's palm and grab the index finger sitting in their palm.

5. Those who don't get their finger grabbed, get the satisfaction of escaping. Those who successfully grab their

neighbor's finger get to celebrate by cheering or waving their hands in the air.

6. Repeat several times.
   - To vary the rules, have students cross their arms with their left hand palm up in front of the person on their right and their right index finger resting in their neighbor's palm.

ⓖ Do Over

(Grade 6–Adult)

In groups of six to eight people, students stand in a circle, facing inward and looking down so that no group member is making eye contact with any other person. Have students count off from one to ten as quickly as possible as they go around the circle. If two people say a number at the same time or if someone's turn is skipped, the next person must start over from one.

ⓖ What Are You Doing?

(Grade 6–Adult)

1. Have small groups of six to eight people stand in a circle. Ask someone to volunteer to start.

2. A volunteer begins to pantomime an easily recognized motion, such as riding a bike, or milking a cow.

3. The person to the left asks, "What are you doing?"

4. While continuing the original pantomime, the first person responds by describing a second activity, for example, "I'm doing jumping jacks."

5. The second person starts doing the named activity (in this example, jumping jacks). As soon as that begins, the first person stands still.

6. As the second person performs the activity, the person on the left asks, "What are you doing?" And so on.

- You could add another element of challenge by having participants keep up their pantomimes even after they have answered the question.

⊚ Buzz Fizz

(Grade 3–Adult)

A large study by Langer (2001) involved teachers to determine which teaching practices most improved test scores. One of the findings was that successful teachers used many different approaches to skill instruction, rather than a single drill or lesson format. Activities such as this one can certainly make learning active, and can provide a different approach to instruction and review.

1. Have all students stand in a circle, facing the center, and number off from left to right.

2. Once everyone has a number, begin to add some layers of complexity. Have them number off again from the same starting point, except this time, a student says "Buzz" when the number is five or a multiple of five: 1, 2, 3, 4, Buzz, 6, 7, 8, 9, Buzz.

3. Add another layer of complexity by introducing a second word (onomatopoeia?) to the counting. For example, use Buzz for multiples of five, and substitute the word Fizz for multiples of seven: 1, 2, 3, 4, Buzz, 6, Fizz, 8, 9, Buzz.

- Instead of using "Buzz" and "Fizz," experiment with different sound effects or words.
- Go around the circle two or three times during the same count instead of stopping it at the starting point.
- Every once in a while change the person who begins, so the students don't get too comfortable with their number.
- Another variation of this would be to have students in small groups, have them turn into the middle of

the circle, and as quickly as they can, have all of their fingers add up to an odd number, say 23. The only rule is that everyone must have at least one finger in.

⊚ Ooh! Ahh! Circle

(Grade 3–Adult)

1. The entire class, including the teacher, stands in a circle holding hands.
2. The teacher starts by squeezing the hand of the student on the right while saying "Ooh."
3. That student squeezes the hand of the person to the right, and says "Ooh."
4. Students pass the squeeze and the "Ooh" to the right until it comes back to the teacher.
5. Next, the teacher squeezes the hand of the student on the left while saying "Ahh."
6. The squeeze and the "Ahh" continue around the circle.
   - To make the game more fun on the second round, the teacher can pick a student to start an "Ooh" in one direction around the circle, and an "Ahh" the other way. Tell the students to watch to see where they collide.

⊚ Bumblebee

(Grade 4–Adult)

Bumblebee is a game that takes place with students sitting in a circle. They could be around a table, or sitting cross-legged on the floor. The students all have an object in front of them. I have adults use their car keys. With younger students, an eraser from their desk will do.

Students repeat this chant: "Lap, clap, bumblebee/lap, clap, grab, slide."

Lap = Pat both hands on lap or on table.

Clap = Clap once.

Bumblebee = Alternate patting hands on lap in time with the words bum-ble-bee (pat right/left/right).

Grab = Students reach with their right hand across their body, and grab the object in front of their neighbor to the left.

Slide = Participants slide the object so it is in front of them.
- Chant is repeated slowly at first, and will naturally pick up speed.
- Switch after a while, and have them reach over their body with their left hand, and grab and slide the object that is in front of the person to their right.

◎ Pass It On

(Grade 4–Adult)

All students stand in a circle. One person starts a single clap, or a pattern of claps. The pattern is then repeated as quickly as possible by everyone in turn around the circle.

Students could send other things around the circle, such as a dance move, an arm movement, an animal sound, or a snort. Challenge the students to pass the sound around the circle as fast as they can.

+ A variation is called "add on." The first student makes a movement, say, a nod of the head. The next person nods their head, then adds on their own movement, such as waving hello, and so on all the way around the circle.

CIRCADIAN RHYTHM

If you are always teaching the same subject at the same time of day, you could be always catching a student on the down side of her particular rhythm, perhaps not getting the best out of that student in that subject. These daily rhythms are called *circadian* rhythms. There are certain times of the day when we naturally have more, and less, energy, depending on the cycle of this circadian rhythm.

There are many different rhythms in the body. Circadian rhythms have cycles of about every 24 hours, *infradian* rhythms relate to cycles less frequent than every 24 hours, and *ultradian* rhythms are more frequent than every 24 hours.

Ultradian rhythms of alternating cerebral dominance have been demonstrated in humans and other mammals while sleeping and awake. When awake, the human cycle is about every 90 minutes (Klein, Pilon, Prosser, & Shannahoff-Khalsa, 1986).

⑤ Mix It Up

(K–Adult)

To take advantage of these natural rhythms, experiment with the following state changes:

+ Try varying the time of day you teach different subjects. What a great state change idea! If your students routinely expect reading first thing in the morning, occasionally change the routine. Some mornings, do math first.
+ You could even have a backwards class. Begin by giving students their homework assignment and saying goodbye, conduct the lesson, and then conclude by correcting the previous day's homework and saying hello.

SILENCE

Our brains need time for unconscious processing. While it is possible for the brain to do two things at once (such as listening to the radio while studying), multitasking diverts energy from the brain's ability to block out distractions. When the brain's attention is divided during the learning of new material, blood flow to the areas of the brain involved in focused attention decreases (Fletcher, Shallice, & Dolan, 1998). For educators, this means that we can have students' attention, and we can facilitate time for them to process the information, but doing both at the same time may not be the best strategy for optimal learning if it is even possible.

Information processing, creating oral responses, and thinking through information can take time. The concept of "think time," as defined by Stahl (1990), would consist of a distinct period of uninterrupted silence by the teacher and all students to give time to complete information processing. Stahl's research showed that students needed at least three seconds of wait time for positive effects to occur.

⑥ "Silent" Processing

(K–Adult)

Having new information introduced before information from the previous lesson is processed and placed into long-term memory can be detrimental to both new learning and old. So, after providing new information, try turning off the music, and telling all of your students to sit down and think, or sit down and write the most important information they just heard.

⑥ Mime Time

(K–Adult)

The brain responds to novelty, and one of the most novel things in a class sometimes can be silence—that is, take things that normally are associated with sound and do them without the sound. Again, this category is only limited by your imagination. You may want to put all ideas into a hat and choose one when the time comes for a little break.

Some ideas include having the kids stand by their desk and doing a silent cheer, silent disco dance, silent boogie, silent yell, silent belly laugh, silent applause, silent hand wave, silent "do the monkey" dance move, silent family reunion, silent "haven't seen you in a long time," silent "you're cool," silent "no, *you're* cool," silent full-body boogie, silent dance like nobody's watching, silent "wiggle absolutely everything until the count of five," and so on.

PRE-WRITING ACTIVITIES

Handwriting is an integral part of every child's school experience. As much as 30 to 60 percent of the elementary school child's class time is spent in fine-motor/writing activities, with writing as the predominant task (McHale & Cermak, 1992).

As important as handwriting is, it is often an overlooked area of school curriculum. It is actually a complex process involving internal factors, such as visual-motor skills, visual perception, and the ability to plan new motor behavior, as well as manipulation of the fine-motor muscles in the hand, and a general kinesthetic awareness (Berninger & Rutberg, 1992; Case-Smith & Pehoski, 1992).

The reasons for paying attention to proper handwriting in children are numerous. For example, handwriting dysfunction among school-aged children is a widespread and significant phenomenon. In one study, researchers (Smits-Engelsman, Van Galen, & Michelis, 1995) reported that 32 percent of the boys and 11 percent of the girls were described by their teachers as having significant handwriting difficulties. In addition, up to 50 percent of students diagnosed with ADHD also have developmental coordination disorder (Flapper, Houwen, & Schoemaker, 2006).

Simple activities such as the ones listed below are great state changes for the entire class. And who knows? They may even help build up the required fine-motor muscles needed for accurate and legible handwriting.

◎ Spider in the Mirror Doing Push-Ups

(K–Grade 5)

The students put their fingers from both hands together, and extend and collapse their fingers, to make it look like a spider on a mirror doing push-ups.

✦ Students find a partner, and do spider in the mirror doing push-ups using one hand from one partner, and the other hand from the other partner.

✦ Spiders can do push-ups anywhere—try on the wall, on a desk, on the side of a neighbor's head, and so forth.

⊚ Mouse Ears

(K–Grade 5)

Students put their hands on the sides of their heads, and alternately extend their fingers (to emulate mouse ears), and scrunch their fingers together, repeating several times.

⊚ Raise the Roof

(K–Grade 5)

Students "raise the roof" by putting their palms up and pushing them toward the ceiling. This would be especially useful if the students did a few pushes with hands straight up, then crossed them over the midline and did some cross-lateral raise the roof. Doing this in rhythm to music could make it especially fun!

A Leg Up

The brain does not store energy, and basically runs on empty. A fresh supply of blood brings it the oxygen and glucose it needs to operate. If the brain does not have enough energy, students become restless, listless, and bored.

Even the simple act of standing up can increase blood flow and improve the brain's ability to pay attention. Standing stimulates the body's adrenal glands and pumps adrenalin into the system. Adrenaline also stimulates the amygdala, the emotional center of the brain.

The role adrenaline plays in enhancing memory was discovered at the University of California at Berkeley (Hatfield & McGaugh, 1999).

Rats put into a tank of water had to swim to find a submerged transparent platform to stand on to rest. Their survival need triggered a rush of adrenaline into their systems. When the rats were returned to the tank after a significant period of time, they easily remembered the location of the transparent resting platform. Rats given beta-blockers (adrenaline-blocking drugs) to neutralize the effects of the adrenaline on their amygdala did not remember the location of the platform.

The benefits of regular activity and exercise are numerous. Exercise increases blood flow and oxygen to the brain, which can increase reaction time. According to Carla Hannaford (1995), physical activity may increase the brain's efficiency, alertness, creativity, and memory, and decrease stress. Exercise and positive social contact have also been shown to increase endorphin levels (Levinthal, 1988). Endorphins are the messengers of our emotional system. They have a positive effect on student behavior in the classroom, because they can reduce pain and increase euphoria (Sylvester, 1994).

All of this from a few jumping jacks? You bet—especially if gross-motor state changes are incorporated on a regular basis into the classroom.

⑨ Calf Pump

(K–Adult)

Second only to the heart, the calf muscles are the best pumps the body has for moving blood through the body and energizing the brain.

+ Have students stand and do 10 to 15 toe lifts. They can lift up on both feet at once, do one set of lifts on the right foot and then on the left foot, or alternate feet for each lift.
+ Have students march in place to John Phillip Sousa's "Stars and Stripes Forever" or the theme from *The Mickey Mouse Club* television show.
+ Do popcorn toe lifts. Start very slowly but gradually increase the frequency until students are doing lots of

toe lifts in rapid succession. Have them finish by gradually slowing down and finally stopping.

✦ Have a vertical jumping contest. See who in your class can jump the highest starting with feet flat on the floor, and jumping straight up using the calf muscles.

⑤ Teach It Standing

(K–Adult)

There is a paradigm that learning takes place seated at a desk. To get kids on their feet and get the blood circulating, have them stand—while you're teaching, while they're reading, when they are discussing material, or use some ways listed below (you may need to adjust the time standing for the younger ones).

✦ Have students give feedback to one another while standing. This is a good way to get blood circulating again, therefore bringing oxygen-rich blood to the brain.

✦ Conduct a classroom review while the students are standing.

✦ During lessons when the class is reading aloud from the same book or packet, have them stand every other page.

⑤ Stand and Stretch

(K–Adult)

Chairs in schools are notoriously uncomfortable. They were not designed for learning; rather, they were designed to stack well. After 20 minutes or so of sitting, students need to move.

✦ Try putting some slow music on, and have students simply stretch, reaching for the sky, touching their toes, and so on. They don't need to do anything fancy—just reach up or rotate at the waist, whatever their body tells them to do.

✦ When the group has done this a few times and feels comfortable, have one person in each group lead the stretch.

✦ Have students do "The Wave" around the classroom. They'll stand up, stretch their arms high, and shout "Whoo!" in a wave-like sequential pattern. This activity can generate lots of excitement and enthusiasm. Let the students stay in motion as long as it continues to be fun.

◎ Hopping Good Time!

(K–Grade 5)

Variations on a hopping theme!

Have all students hop together three times (or any other number of times you choose).

✦ Hop on one foot, hop on the other foot.
✦ Hop on balls of feet.
✦ Hop all the way around in three hops.
✦ Turn 180 degrees, or even 360 degrees each hop.
✦ Hop as high as you can.
✦ Hop as low as you can.
✦ Hop as fast as you can.
✦ Hop as many times as you can in five seconds.
✦ If students are in a small group, have them put their arms around each other's shoulders and do a group hop seven times.

Add your own ideas—come on, hop to it!

◎ Jumping Jacks

(K–Grade 12)

In this activity, the teacher (or active student) leads the class in a predetermined number of jumping jacks.

✦ "Swat the fly" (just jump up as high as you can and clap hands together at apex of jump).
✦ Have a contest to see how many jumping jacks students can complete in 20 seconds.
✦ Do a 90- or 180-degree turn with every jumping jack.

⑤ "Do Do, Run Run"

(K–Grade 5)

Students stand by their desk and run in place until a count of 10, or some other predetermined number. Have them

✦ Run as fast as they can.
✦ Run with knees as high up as they can go.
✦ Run as slowly as they can.
✦ Run while pantomiming a scene is being narrated, wave at people, splash water on your face—put the score from the film *Chariots of Fire* on while doing this—it is hilarious!
✦ Run in place without moving their arms.
✦ Run in place, moving their arms as if they are running, but without the feet moving.

⑤ Hi There, Pop!

(K–Grade 5)

✦ Have students make popping sounds with their mouths. Have them start slowly, then go faster, and then slow down again, like they are popping popcorn.
✦ Have students be popcorn kernels in their seats, using their legs to pop up and down slowly while making popping sounds with their mouths, then more quickly to match the sounds.
✦ I have done this with the sound of popping corn from a sound effects CD I found at my local library.

⊚ Sounds Moving . . .

(K–Grade 12)

To facilitate transitions that are enjoyable, memorable, and effective, try this state change idea. As students are walking from one place to another during a transition, ask students to make a predetermined sound every time their feet hit the floor while they are walking. For example:

+ Left foot, Ooh! Right foot, Ahh!
+ Sound like you're walking in mud.
+ Sound like you're on top of angry cows, and so on.

GROSS MOTOR

With the ubiquitous presence of computers, video games, and the like, students today often get more stimulation of their fine-motor muscles than their gross-motor muscles. If they have difficulty with their gross-motor muscles, they could feel clumsy or awkward when doing physical tasks, even running and playing. This may lead to avoiding such activities, resulting in a great deficit in the amount that the body and brain are connected together and working and communicating smoothly with each other.

Another area of concern connected with the lack of gross-motor activities for many of today's youth concerns the neurotransmitter *dopamine.* When dopamine is in your body, you feel good. As a matter of fact, it is not the drug cocaine that gives the user a feeling of euphoria. The cocaine triggers an enormous release of dopamine into your system. The basal ganglia are part of the system in the brain that produces dopamine.

The basal ganglia are a set of structures buried deep within the brain that are involved with the control and sequencing of movement. Parts of the basal ganglia include the caudate nucleus and the lenticular nucleus, located in front of the thalamus in each cerebral hemisphere. This area of the brain acts like a relay station, receiving connections from the motor areas of the cortex that are responsible for organizing movement commands, and receiving connections from the dopamine-producing cells at the base of the brain where it connects to the spinal cord. This particular part of the brain stem, which produces dopamine, is known as the substantia nigra, another part of the basal ganglia. The cells of the substantia nigra connect to the cells in the relay station where dopamine is released.

I find it fascinating that the areas responsible for, and stimulated by, body movement also control the production and release of dopamine. Is it possible that the rise in the use of antidepressants, especially in young children, could be partly rooted in a lack of gross-motor movement?

If lack of gross-motor movement can be detrimental to a student's overall health and success, the good news is that regular gross-motor stimulation has positive benefits.

Movement increases heart rate and circulation and triggers arousal mechanisms. Activities that include spinning and body rotation, like dance moves, may be essential to the formation of critical brain areas responsible for controlling spatial, visual, auditory, and motor functions (Palmer, 1980). When dance and movement are used in the classroom, the emotions released stimulate the amygdala, the brain's emotional center, which is important in the memory process. Combining dance, creative movement, and fine arts with classroom learning can improve students' self-image, motor coordination, and stress response.

Trying the following state changes will stimulate your students' attentional systems. It may also have the added benefit of releasing dopamine and improving the overall positive mood of individual students, and the overall positive climate of the class.

⑥ Hand to Fist

(Grade 3–Adult)

Hand to fist is like playing a game of patty-cake but with a crafty twist.

I divide this game into three levels of difficulty (you may not get through all three levels of difficulty with younger students).

Level One

+ In pairs, students stand facing each other.
+ One partner holds up two fists, the other partner holds up two open palms.
+ They push their palms and fists toward each other, then bring them away and switch. The partner with the palms now makes fists, and the partner that had the fists now opens his palms, and they push their hands together again. This is repeated several times with increasing speed.

Level Two

+ Partners face each other.
+ Each partner makes a fist with the right hand and holds up the left hand with the palm open. Slowly at first, the partners push their hands together so that palm meets fist and fist meets palm. They pull their hands apart and switch.

Level Three

+ Level Three is the same as Level Two, with one exception. Instead of pushing palms and fists together at the same time, the partners alternate right and then left hand, palm to fist. Then they pull their hands apart, switch—palm becomes fist, fist becomes palm—and partners push hands together again.

☺ Musical Tables

(K–Grade 12)

A very quick state change that can get the blood flowing! Simply have the students stand up, and direct them to walk around their tables until the music stops.

+ Have students walk around room, media center, and so forth. Or, if it's a nice day, take your class on a walk around the school, playground, or parking lot. (This is also a great way to stimulate dopamine production.)

+ Another innovation is to play the song "Dizzy" by Tommy Roe, and have the students walk around their chairs a few times.

+ What a fun way to do a review for a test! Whoever gets left without a chair must answer a test review question.

◎ Hand Jive

(Grade 4–Adult)

This is the hand jive that was popular in the golden age of rock and roll. Any peppy, up-tempo piece of music will work as accompaniment, but "Willie and the Hand Jive" by Johnny Otis or "Born to Hand Jive" from the soundtrack of the musical *Grease* are both particularly fun to use.

In case you don't know the hand jive, the motions are listed here. It is a 16-beat pattern and moves very fast!

Students can do the traditional hand jive either sitting or standing.

1. Pat your lap twice.

2. Clap twice.

3. With your palms facing down, cross your hands in the air twice. Cross your hands twice in the air again, this time with the other hand on top.

4. Bounce one fist on the other twice. Bounce the fists twice again, this time with the other fist on top.

5. With the right hand, jerk a hitchhiker thumb over the right shoulder twice. With the left hand, jerk a hitchhiker thumb over the left shoulder twice.

   • Have students, individually or in a group, make up their own hand jives, coming up with 16 counts of movement. Students can then perform their creations for the class.

◎ Stand on One Foot

(K–Grade 5)

To help stimulate the vestibular system, which is our sense of balance, have students try standing on one foot until the count of 10, or turn it into a competition to see who can stand on one foot the longest.

+ Try standing on one foot with both eyes closed.
+ Try standing on one foot with both arms outstretched to the side.
+ Try standing on one foot with both arms out to the side and both eyes closed.
+ Try standing on one foot with both arms out to the side, eyes open, and head tilted back looking up at the ceiling.

If a student absolutely cannot do this, or does it only with great difficulty, there may be issues with his or her vestibular system. Maybe your school's occupational therapist can come in with the parents' permission for an informal observation. Chances are, that child has difficulty reading as well.

◎ Muscle Poses

(K–Adult)

The teacher models a choice of three different muscle poses, and on the count of three, all students make one and hold with a Grrrrr. Choices could include

+ "The Crab" (bending over slightly, fists together by belly button).
+ "The Double Bicep" (both hands up in the air, elbows bent, showing off biceps).
+ "The Hero" (palms flat, fingers tight together, one arm bent with hand behind ear, the other arm locked straight, held out to the side, head looking up at stiff hand, hero style!).

Having muscles contract as they do in these muscle poses is a form of resistance training, which has been shown to be an effective and efficient way to exercise muscles and build strength (Ariel, 1978). Your students who are extroverts will love the possibilities in this activity to ham it up! This activity is especially fun if you put on inspirational music like "Eye of the Tiger" or the theme song from the movie *Rocky*.

EYES

Vision is critical to success in school. So many of the activities in school are vision related, or vision dependent, that the importance of a properly functioning visual system cannot be overlooked.

Vision is more that just 20/20 eyesight. I break the visual system down into two parts—the visible and the invisible. The visible part of the visual system includes the visible structures of the eye, and what is controlled visibly by muscles in and around the eye. Skills such as distance and near acuity, focusing, along with eye movement skills such as pursuits (which are smooth eye movements), and saccades (which are the jerky little eye movements we use when we read), are some of the skills present in the visible part of the visual system we use constantly in school. When the visual signal travels down the optic nerve into the occipital lobe in the brain located in the back of the head, this is what I refer to as the invisible portion of the visual system. The signal gets to the brain, and we cannot directly observe how those signals are processed. Even though we cannot see what happens, there are many visual perceptual skills such as figure-ground (which is the ability to pick a specific figure or object out of a background of other objects, like finding your paper amongst all the ones hanging on the bulletin board), and form constancy (which is knowing that the letter "a" is still the letter "a," whether it is in Arial font or Times Roman font), that all take place in the brain, and all have a part in the reading process.

Research has indicated (Birnbaum, 1993) that vision disorders frequently interfere with reading and learning. Often, vision tests in school only screen for distance visual acuity, to make sure students can see clearly 20 feet away. The irony is most vision-related tasks in schools are near-vision tasks. In addition, there are many other eye skills that are needed for success in school. Activities described below may help develop visual skills, and if students are not able to do these tasks, it may be an indicator of a problem that should be diagnosed and treated.

Visual skills are extremely important for any student's optimal learning. Although visual problems have been noted in regular education students, there is an even greater incidence of vision problems in learning disabled populations (Hoffman, 1980). Activities such as those included in this section could help some students, and perhaps students with learning disabilities the most.

⑨ You're Getting Sleeeeeeeepy . . .

(K–Grade 5)

An important eye movement skill is called fixation, which is the eye's ability to fixate or stare at an object. This is an important skill in school, especially for reading. As the eye moves across a page with its saccadic movement, the eye does not register information. The instant that the saccade stops, however, the eyes must immediately fixate on the letter, word, or group of words they encounter. If the eyes have difficulty fixating on a line of text, reading becomes very difficult, students lose their place while reading, and fluency rate goes down. The following activity can be a fun state change, can help students with the eye skill of fixation, and may even be useful as an informal screening for certain vision problems.

When students need a quick break, have them pick out an object, or even a spot on a wall or on their desk, and when the teacher says, "Go," see if they can stare at it without looking away for 30 seconds. They can blink—just not look away.

✦ You could have students pair up and monitor each other, as students are sometimes not self-aware enough to notice quick glances away from the target.

⑥ The Corner of Your Eye

(K–Grade 5)

Having a normal field of peripheral vision is essential for optimal success in school. Peripheral stimuli help make us aware of our surroundings, can help with memory processes, keep us safe, and help us to read. When we read, we detect words and images with our peripheral vision, and that helps us read faster and more accurately with better comprehension.

Have students look straight ahead, and see how many objects they can see with their peripheral vision.

✦ You could have them find objects of a certain color, try to determine the color of their neighbor's shirt, and so on.
✦ Try pairing students up, and have each partner in turn hold up objects or a number of fingers that the other student must identify using only peripheral vision.

⑥ Saccades

(K–Grade 5)

Saccades are rapid, jerky eye movements that are made as you read across a line of text. Having both eyes working together as a unit and stopping and starting together is a skill that good readers share. If a student does not have adequate saccadic movement, they may be slow readers with poor comprehension. They may lose their place often while they are reading, and as a result, may not like to read out loud. Vision therapists are extremely clever in ways to improve the efficiency of saccadic eye movements.

Have students look at something that is displayed across the front of the room. It could be an alphabet strip, a number line, or a series of objects. Direct them to keep their heads still, then find and focus on certain objects you mention as quickly as they can. You could also clap a steady beat or put on a metronome, and have them switch back and forth between the targets with their eyes, keeping their head still on the beat.

✦ Teachers can also have students hold up both of their hands, palms toward them, and ask students to look back and forth between their palms while keeping their heads still.

✦ Students could also hold up cards, such as flashcards, in each hand, and read the cards back and forth.

✦ The teacher could also have two flashlights and ask students to look back and forth between the beams.

⊚ Spin It!

(K–Grade 5)

The visual system is tied into our vestibular sense, which tells us where we are in three-dimensional space. For example, there is something called the *vestibular-occular reflex,* which is how our vestibular system keeps our vision steady, even when we are walking or running. There are three semi-circular canals in the inner ear that roughly equate to our three planes of movement—horizontally, vertically, and rotationally. Spinning activities with all of the variations mentioned below stimulate all of these sensors.

✦ Students stand next to their desks and spin in a tight circle, two or three times one way, two or three times the other way.

✦ Turn with eyes open, and with eyes shut (with eyes shut, caution them about moving safely and more slowly).

✦ Other variations: Spin with arms out (if room allows), spin with head down (chin on chest), or spin with head up (eyes looking at ceiling).

◎ Starfish/Octopus

(K–Grade 5)

Optometrists call the eye's ability to adjust its focus from near to far the skill of accommodation. Accommodation results from the contraction or relaxation of small muscles in the eye called the cilliary muscles. When these cilliary muscles contract, the eye's crystalline lens is slightly squashed. For viewing distant objects, the cilliary muscles relax and the eye's crystalline lens is stretched out. When this accommodation skill is working properly, the eye can focus and refocus quickly and effortlessly. There may be more students with accommodation problems than there were a generation ago, simply because of the vast number of hours students today often are looking at stationary objects at a fixed distance, such as a television, computer screens, or hand-held gaming devices, and not exercising their cilliary muscles.

(Just as an aside, the ability of the eye to accommodate does decrease with age due to the crystalline lens becoming less flexible causing a condition called presbyopia. That's what I got as a 40th birthday present. Presbyopia. Great.)

To help practice near focus and far focus, and to widen students' visual field, try this fun activity.

1. Tell students to spread their fingers on one hand and put it about 12 inches away from their eyes. Have them stare at the hand.

2. Have them focus on the back of their hand first—that's the "starfish."

3. Then, ask them to keep looking at their hand, but focus on the floor or desk behind their hand. They will see the "ghost fingers" as well as their own fingers—that's the "octopus."

4. Have them practice going back and forth between starfish and octopus several times.
   • Have them try it one eye at a time, with the other eye closed.

⑥ The Amazing Floating Sausage

(K–Adult)

This is another activity that will exercise the students' eye muscles that work on focusing—so essential for a fluent reader.

1. To see the floating sausage have students point their index fingers at each other about four to six inches in front of their face.

2. As they slowly bring the fingers toward each other, have them focus beyond the fingers, like they did in "Starfish/Octopus." They will see a little "sausage" floating, made out of tips of each of their index fingers. Very cool!

   • Have your students start with one finger on each hand. Once they have mastered the soft focus needed to see the finger sausage, have them try it with two fingers on each hand, then three, and even four fingers on each hand for a floating sausage extravaganza.

   • The closer the fingers are to the face, the bigger the sausage will appear. See if students can start off with their fingers closer to their face, then keep the sausage in focus as they move their fingers away, making the sausage smaller.

⑥ Hot Hands

(Grade 3–Adult)

Like any other muscles in the body, the eyes can get tired after working for extended periods of time. The muscles used to move the eyes, and the cilliary muscles used to focus the eyes, can get fatigued if reading or doing close-up work for extended periods of time.

To give eyes a rest, have your students rub their hands together until the hands feel warm, then place their palms over their eyes. Make sure they are not applying undue pressure to their eyes, and instruct them to simply relax for a moment, letting their eyes enjoy the warmth and darkness.

Repeating a few times is recommended.

+ Another way to relax the eyes is to focus on a distant object to relax the cilliary muscles that are used for focusing. You could make this part of your classroom routine—every hour, take a 20-second eye break and focus on something distant outside the classroom window.

+ Teachers could also ask their students to blink several times to make sure their eyes stay moist.

◉ Follow That Finger

(Grades 3–6)

Keeping their heads still, have students follow their neighbor's finger with their eyes as it slowly moves side to side, up and down, diagonally, and in circles around their face.

An important visual skill is the ability to have our eyes smoothly follow a moving target. These smooth pursuit movements require the absolute precise coordination of the six muscles in each eye. The order that the pursuits are suggested—horizontally, vertically, diagonally, and rotationally—coincide with the developmental stages of these pursuit movements. If students find that they or their partners are not able to smoothly follow in one of these directions, it may indicate an oculomotor, or eye muscle, issue, which usually can be handled with a referral to a professional vision therapist.

◉ Jump the Ring!

(Grade 3–Adult)

I have always found that students are fascinated to find out more about themselves. Students usually know they have a dominant hand, but often don't know they have other dominate senses as well, such as a dominant eye. To discover which of their eyes is dominant, have your students complete the following steps:

1. Make a circle with their thumb and forefinger.
2. With both eyes, look through the circle at an object.
3. While continuing to look through the circle, have them close one eye at a time. When one eye is closed, the object will jump out of the circle; when the other eye is closed, the object will stay in the circle. The eye that keeps the object in the circle is the student's dominant eye.

Students will usually have a dominant eye. One thing to be aware of is if the non-dominant eye is very weak. The brain may suppress the incoming signal from the weak eye, making the dominant eye work even harder. The wise teacher will notice if a student consistently tears up or rubs one particular eye. It could mean the student needs vision therapy or perhaps glasses to strengthen the non-dominant eye and gain an optimally functioning visual system.

⊚ The Trombone

(K–Grade 5)

Another way for students to practice near and far focus is to have them hold one hand up by their face, as if holding onto a trombone slide. Instruct them to slowly move the hand toward and away from their face, while keeping their hand in focus.

✦ Try with both eyes, then with each eye shut in turn.

⊚ The Pen Is Mighty Indeed

(Grade 3–Adult)

Here is a fun little activity to check for stereopsis, or depth perception. If a child cannot do this activity, it may be that parents should be alerted. Perhaps they will wish to have an optometrist check for depth perception issues.

Take two pens, one in each hand, and hold them out at arms length. With one eye closed, try to bring the pen tips together so they touch. Try it with the other eye closed as well. You should be fairly accurate in getting the pen tips to touch. If you or any of your students are off consistently, or by a wide margin, it might suggest that a trip to the eye doctor would be in order.

PROPS

Every attempt has been made to limit the activities in this book to those not requiring any props, just to make the activities as "in the moment" as possible. However, using the occasional prop can help bolster some students' confidence as having something in their hands can be a bit soothing.

Some studies (Jacobs & Nadel, 1985) indicate that short-term memory, and the brain's ability to create new long-term memories, are inhibited under stressful conditions. So holding a prop may help a student relax in the present and remember better in the future.

◎ Hula Hoop Pass

(Grades 4–12)

1. Students stand in a circle of six to eight members.

2. Students join hands.

3. A hula hoop is given to the group, with the instructions to pass the hula hoop around the circle, without letting go of hands. Students bend, wiggle, step on, and use their heads to get the hula hoop going around.
   - Add an element of competition to the activity by racing against the clock or another group.
   - Fun can also be had by placing several hula hoops at once in a circle, all going in the same direction, or going in different directions.

⊚ Beach Ball Sharing

(Grades 3–12)

The teacher tosses a beach ball around to students. The beach ball has different discussion categories written in each of the colored sections. Whichever section the students see when they catch the ball provides the word or topic on which they should speak. Possible topics could be

+ Describe how you are feeling right now.
+ Tell the class one thing you have learned so far this semester.
+ Tell the class about the kind of person you are in a group.

⊚ Beach Ball Brainstorm

(Grade 3–Adult)

The teacher decides a category and announces the category to the class. For example, the teacher could pick ideas like

+ Things that are round.
+ Cartoon characters.
+ Compliments.
+ Things that are sweet.
+ Jungle animals, and so on.

The teacher begins by saying something in that category, then passes the beach ball or object to someone else in class. To lower the risk, students could raise their hands if they have an idea and the ball or object is only passed to the people with their hands raised. This activity can bring a lot of laughs, is a good brain stretch, and can be a fun bonding experience.

⊚ Clay Charades

(Grade 6–Adult)

A great game to play with Play-Doh or clay is charades. One person in a group looks at a word that the teacher has written on a piece of paper, and tries to create that object out of clay. The rest of the group is trying to guess the object more quickly than any other group.

✦ I try to provide some weird ideas just to make the students laugh. Words that I have used in the past include dandruff, brick wall, keyhole, jellyfish, lottery ticket, belly button lint, and toe nail, to name a few.

✦ This could also be a fun review, using vocabulary words from a recent unit. For example, if you are teaching science, words could include mitosis, photosynthesis, and so on.

◎ Ball Toss

(Grade 6–Adult)

This can be a great deal of fun, an excellent state change activity, and an interactive way to review. Students stand in a circle, and begin tossing a ball or object around the circle. Each person receives the object only once. Students must remember the pattern—they must pay attention to who threw the object to them, and who they threw it to next.

✦ Another fun thing to do is to prepare several objects for each group. Have students create a pattern with the first object, then start adding more objects to the group juggle one at a time, until the group is tossing four to five objects all at once.

◎ Balloons Up!

(Grade 4–Adult)

1. Students form a circle of six to eight people.

2. Everyone in the circle reaches in and grabs the hands of two other people.

3. Toss one or more balloons (inflated with air, not helium) into each circle; the groups are required to keep the balloons aloft without letting go of each other's hands.
   - Spice up the game by adding rules along the lines of no person is allowed to hit the balloon twice in a row or the student must name a fact from the previous lesson each time they hit a balloon.
   - To vary the activity, give students helium balloons and instruct them to keep the balloons from floating to the ceiling.

⊚ String Squares

(Grades 3–8)

1. Students get into groups of six to eight.

2. Each group is given a string or piece of yarn, approximately 10- to 15-feet long.

3. The teacher asks students to make particular shapes with the string, for example, a triangle, square, rectangle, octagon, pentagon, trapezoid, and so forth. Some shapes may even have more points than there are people in the group.
   - Variations include doing this with eyes shut or blindfolded, or with groups not allowed to speak.

PART 4

Build Teams and Community

*O*ne of the 12 mind/brain learning principles highlighted by Geoffrey and Renate Caine (Caine, Caine, & Crowell, 1999) is the idea that we are social beings, and we learn in a social context. When I think of this brain principle, I am reminded how important positive social interaction is when creating the optimal learning environment. In modern society, those who break the law can go to prison. Prisoners who do not comply get into trouble, and sometimes they are sent to solitary confinement. Solitary confinement is considered a punishment for our worst offenders. Yet when I think back to my years of schooling, I think of how much was done individually, with no talking allowed, in an isolated setting.

The ability to create a classroom community infused with high challenge, low threat, and high support is essential for effective educators. According to Hirschi (1969), social bonding consists of four basic elements: attachment, commitment, involvement, and belief. Attachment is the strength of ties to others, commitment is the investment in conventional activities, involvement is the proportion of time spent in conventional activities, and belief is the conviction that the norms expected by society for good behavior are just and true.

Hirschi (1969) believed that adolescents that are bonded to others, such as teachers and other students, and even institutions such as school, will not act out because they fear losing the positive connection they have with those individuals or the institution. This is a powerful way of saying that not only can learning increase with positive student bonding, but classroom management may be positively affected as well.

Research has indicated that if adolescents are bonded to, attached to, committed to, and involved in a group through conventional social activities, it decreases the likelihood that students will engage in risk taking, and potential harmful activities (McBride et al., 1995). This study even goes so far as to predict the future success of ninth graders in the study, based on the amount of bonding opportunities they had in school.

Negative adolescent behavior, including substance abuse, truancy, and school misconduct, are common concerns. One recent study of middle school students found that students who developed positive social bonds with their classmates and teachers were more likely to perform well academically. Positive social bonds also reduced the amount of misconduct and antisocial behavior (Simons-Morton, Crump, Haynie, & Saylor, 1999). Simple activities such as the ones in this section can help refresh students' attention, and can increase the positive bond students feel with one another, resulting in many positive benefits.

Does it make a difference if the students are familiar with the instructor? It seem reasonable to assume that students would feel more relaxed in a classroom environment where they knew the teacher, but would it make a difference instructionally? According to one study (van Driel & Talling, 2005), test animals actually scored consistently higher on tasks when they were familiar with the experimenters. If the test animals were unfamiliar with the experimenters, they consistently did poorly on the tests. It stands to reason that activities such as those in this section can help students get to know their teachers a little better, can be beneficial for building teacher and student rapport, and perhaps have an impact on the learning as well.

Research has indicated (MacElveen-Hoehn & Eyres, 1984) that positive interactions of adults and children, and positive interactions with members of their social networks, such as their classmates, are important in the development of essential cognitive and social skills, as well as for the promotion of security and comfort.

Activities such as the ones included in this section can support creating the conditions where positive social interactions can take place, for the benefit of the individual, and the good of the entire class.

GETTING TO KNOW YOU

☺ Handshakes

(K–Adult)

Social competence is the single best predictor of success in adulthood (Feehan, McGee, Williams, & Nada-Raja, 1995). Students with antisocial behavior, such as difficulty regulating emotions or maintaining close friendships, are at greater risk for dropping out of school or developing mental health problems later in life.

Early intervention, in a fun, non-threatening way, may mitigate some of these problems. Activities like the ones below can directly and indirectly teach students some of the social skills required to participate in their community.

+ When students complete an activity, have them shake each other's hands in different ways. Some fun handshakes are:
  1. Farmer handshakes: One person (the cow) extends his fingers, the other person (the farmer) "milks" the fingers of the outstretched hand.
  2. Fisherman handshakes: One person extends her hand, the other person grabs the fingers, and uses the thumb of the hand like a fishing reel, winding the thumb gently around like reeling in a fish.

3. Shake with left hands, pinky shakes, and so on.
4. Fingertip handshake: Put fingertips of both hands together and wiggle.
5. Musical handshakes: One person squeezes out the rhythm of a familiar song. Students may sit down when they both guess each other's song.

    Sample songs are "Twinkle, Twinkle Little Star," "Mary Had a Little Lamb," "Jingle Bells," and so on. This is another great kinesthetic state change, as well as a way to increase positive affirmations and build community.
6. Individual students could invent their own handshakes and teach them to five other people before sitting down, or use their new handshake as they introduce themselves to five new people before sitting down. Alternately, small groups invent a handshake and demonstrate it to the rest of the class

◎ Simon Says

(K–Adult)

Try playing this perennial favorite with your class.

+ Use it as a listening game for following instructions.
+ Use as a get-to-know-you game: For example, Simon Says point to someone you have just met and say her name out loud.
+ Use as a geography game: Simon Says point in the direction of Alaska.
+ Use as a math game: Simon Says use your body to give the answer to 5 plus 6.
+ Language learning: Simon Says point to *la playa*.
+ A science game: Simon Says point to something in this room made of steel, made of glass, made of plastic, that's over 20 years old, that would have not existed 50 years ago.

⑥ Meet Three People Who . . .

(Grade 4–Adult)

Have all students stand up, and shake hands with three people who . . .

- ✦ Are wearing blue.
- ✦ Have ever been out of the country.
- ✦ Have the same shoe size you have, plus or minus a half size.
- ✦ Have ever been on a cruise.
- ✦ Have the same number of siblings.
- ✦ And so on, asking low-gradient getting-to-know-you questions.

⑥ GLP Walk

(Grade 6–Adult)

1. Stand up.

2. Pick a partner.

3. Give students a time limit, usually about seven to nine minutes, to walk with their partner and take turns talking about G-L-P.

   "G" stands for something they are *grateful* for.

   "L" stands for something they have *learned*, maybe in this class, maybe in life.

   "P" stands for a *promise* they are going to make to themselves—perhaps that this will be the best class ever, or that they will actively participate more than ever before.

When I do this with a class, I like to change the questions after a few weeks to keep things fresh. Some ideas to share are

- ✦ Three things you've learned in this class.

✦ Two things you learned from this class that you've used in real life.

✦ One question you still have about the material we are studying.

⑤ Enrolling Questions

(Grade 6–Adult)

Enrolling questions are low-threat, easily answered questions presented to the entire group about any topic. They allow everyone to participate without the stress of being put on the spot in front of their peers.

✦ Teacher says: "Raise your hand if your eyes are blue."

✦ Teacher asks everyone to stand, then says: "Sit down if you have at least a size five shoe." (Keep going to see who has the largest shoe size in the class.)

✦ Teacher says: "Please move to the right side of the room if you have ever traveled out of the country." (Find out who went the farthest.)

✦ Teacher says: "Stand up if you have ever been on a cruise." (Find out what destinations students visited.)

✦ Ask the group to come up with questions to ask the rest of the group, and then give them the opportunity to ask. Set the parameters at the beginning of this activity, so they know it can't be anything too personal or revealing.

✦ Rather than give out a lengthy list of your qualifications, have the students ask questions about you; for example, where you went to college, whether you have any brothers or sisters, why you started teaching, and so on.

⑤ Brave New Words

(Grade 6–Adult)

Display on an overhead transparency or large poster a list of words that describe positive moods (see examples below).

Instruct each student to choose a word that either describes how she is feeling, or perhaps how she wants to feel. Students are then given time to introduce themselves to everyone in the room, using their chosen word in the greeting. For example "Hi, my name's Jerry, and I'm feeling groovy!"

Some sample words:

Great, groovy, wonderful, magnificent, superb, splendid, glorious, brilliant, outstanding, stupendous, dazzling, sanguine, confident, optimistic, cheerful, ecstatic, blissful, elated, delighted, euphoric, jubilant, astounding, amazing, stunning, spectacular, cool, hip, harmonious, astonishing.

⊚ Let's Shake On It

(Grade 4–Adult)

Student pairs stand facing each other, reach out and grab each other's hand as if they are about to shake hands. When the teacher says, "Go," the students are instructed to try to get their partner's hand over to touch their hip. If they succeed, they get a point. The teacher may instruct the class to go for one minute and see which partner has the highest score.

The point of this exercise is that if both partners work together, they can simply go back and forth, moving their hands from hip to hip countless times, resulting in a win for both of them.

⊚ True/False Test

(Grade 3–Adult)

The teacher creates a true/false test about himself or herself. As the questions are revealed one at a time, the students stand up or raise a hand if they believe the statement is true about the instructor. The students then get a chance to create three or four true/false questions about themselves. The teacher asks a few students a day to have the rest of the class guess which statements are true, and which statements are false.

⊚ Archeological Dig

(Grade 3–Adult)

The teacher gives students a time frame, say, 10 minutes, to complete a secret mission. That mission is to become archeologists, and to "uncover" three facts about as many people as possible in the classroom. When the dig is over, class members get a chance to read the facts they uncovered, while the rest of the class tries to guess who the mystery person is.

⊚ Bring It On!

(Grade 3–Adult)

Students are asked to find an object in the classroom or their desk, or to bring an object from home that represents something about them. Time is then given in small or large groups to share the object and the story that goes with it.

⊚ We Like to Move It

(Grade 4–Adult)

1. The entire class forms a huddle in the middle of an open area. Teacher brings a portable CD or cassette player and some upbeat, bouncy, instrumental music, perhaps "Hit Me Up" from the *Happy Feet* soundtrack.

2. When the music begins, students drop their heads and hands, keep their eyes on the ground, and shuffle around close to each other, while chanting, "We like to move it, move it."

3. When the music is paused, students stop their shuffling and wait for instructions from the teacher.

4. The teacher gives the group a direction, such as, "Touch two pieces of jewelry closest to you," "Touch two items the color blue," "Touch a white shoe," "Put your right elbow on someone's knee," "Put your left hand on someone's shoe," and so forth. Students may have to search to find the designated object or color.

5. Turn the music back on and have students again shuffle around, until you stop the music and give them the next set of instructions.

☺ Two Truths and a Lie

(Grade 6–Adult)

1. Put students in small groups, and have them think of two things that are true about them, and one thing that is untrue. Encourage the students to come up with truths that perhaps no one knows about, or that seem outrageous.

2. In their small groups, each person takes a turn stating, in any order, the two truths and a lie.

3. Group members try to guess which statements are true, and which one is false.

Scientists at the University of Pennsylvania used fMRI technology (functional magnetic resonance imaging) to show that blood flow increases to different areas of the brain when someone is lying. Subjects who answered questions falsely activated the anterior cingulate gyrus and the left pre-motor cortex regions of the brain, which are responsible for attention, judgment, and the detection of errors (Langleben, Austin, Goris, & Strauss, 2001).

☺ That's Quite a Yarn!

(Grade 4–Adult)

1. Greet students at the door with a bundle of yarn and a pair of scissors.

2. As students enter the classroom, cut them a length of yarn as long as they want, but don't tell them what the yarn is for.

3. Seat students in small groups and have them choose a temporary leader.

4. Instruct the group leaders to wrap their piece of yarn around one of their fingers. While they are wrapping the yarn, they share aloud some personal information with their group. Offer some topic suggestions to help them get started; they can talk about how many siblings or children they have, their favorite food or movie, or even professional goals and ambitions.

5. They keep talking until the yarn is entirely wound around a finger, then the next person in their group begins to wrap and rap.
   - Try doing the same thing with a roll of toilet paper. Every student coming in the room can take as many squares of toilet paper as he or she desires. When it is time for the activity, they find that they must tell the class one fact about themselves for every square of toilet paper they have in their possession.
   - Try giving the students M&M's candies. Students are instructed to not eat the candies, but can take as many as they can hold in one hand. When students are seated, have them share with the class or the group types of information according to the candy colors. For example, for every brown M&M, tell the class something you like about school. For every red M&M, tell the class something you like to do in your spare time, and so on.

⑤ Motion Potion

(Grade 3–Adult)

Because this activity stores information in multiple pathways by being auditory, visual, and kinesthetic, I have found it to be an excellent tool for learning and remembering names at the start of a course.

1. The entire class stands in a circle.

2. Students say their name, along with an aptly descriptive adjective with the same beginning sound as their

first name, for example, Jazzy Jerry, Funny Fiona, Kicking Kelly. As they are saying their names, students will also make a unique motion with their hands; for example, Talkative Teresa might open and close her hands like she's talking.

3. After students say their names, everyone in the circle repeats the adjective and name, and mimics the motion.

4. The activity continues until everyone has had a turn.

◎ Human Bingo

(Grade 3–Adult)

The teacher has students fill out an informational card, asking for things that their classmates may not know about each other. The teacher creates a bingo card that asks the questions, and the students go around and try to find a classmate who matches the square.

✦ Alternatively, the teacher could pass out bingo cards with pre-prepared statements, such as "I have been on a cruise," "I have a pet," "I have ridden on a roller coaster," "I have at least one sister," "I have brown eyes," and the students find one of their classmates for whom this is true, and have their classmate initial that square.

✦ To learn names at the beginning of the year, have students walk around with a blank bingo card, and have them ask their fellow students their names. Then have students write their names on a card. The teacher then puts everyone's name in a hat and uses the cards to play bingo.

◎ All My Neighbors

(Grade 6–Adult)

This game has turned into one of my favorites over the years. All students sit in a circle, with enough chairs for all students except for one. The one student standing goes to the middle of the circle and asks a question, worded like this: "I love all my neighbors, especially those who have a pet." Students who have a pet must stand up and sit in a different chair, at least one chair away from their own. The one person who remains standing then goes to the middle of the circle and asks the next question. Try it and see what happens.

⑥ Purse, Wallet, Backpack, or Desk

(Grade 6–Adult)

Students have a time limit, say, one minute, to find something in their purse, wallet, backpack, or desk that says something about who they are or what they believe in. The object and the story that goes with it are then shared in large or small groups. The teacher needs to give some examples of what is appropriate, for example, a picture of people that are important to you, your voter registration card, a charm or medallion that has significance. The teacher should be explicit about what is appropriate and not appropriate for sharing in a group.

⑥ What Is Your Nickname?

(Grade 4–Adult)

Students share their nickname, and the story behind how they got that nickname. If they don't have one, ask them what would they like it to be.

⑥ Superpower

(K–Adult)

Students are asked if they could have a superpower, what would it be? Flight? Invisibility? Strength? Or something more unusual, like the ability to milk cows at a distance? The ability to make flies dizzy? The ability to always get the coupon price, even though you don't have the coupon? The ability to make someone's clothes feel wet?

The superpower and the story behind it get shared in large or small groups.

◎ This Is a Picture of Myself When I Was Younger

(K–Adult)

Students and teacher bring in pictures of themselves. Possibilities include

+ Baby pictures.
+ Picture of you having a great time.
+ Picture of you at an important event in your life.
+ Picture of you and at least one important person in your life (must say why).
+ Picture of you with big hair.
+ Picture of you with your first car (for older students or adults).

◎ Visible Scar Activity

(Grade 6–Adult)

This is one I came up with one night in class, and it has been a hit every single time I have used it. I simply ask the students if they have any visible scars, and to please share the stories about how they got them. I haven't ever needed to say anything about confidentiality, for example, if a student were to show a scar from an abusive situation, although I have used this mainly with adults. With high school students, I would probably make a general announcement to share only what students are comfortable with, and as teacher, I have ultimate veto power to stop a story immediately if I think it is going someplace I don't want to go.

◎ The Year of the Penny

(Grade 6–Adult)

Pennies are passed out, and students share something significant that happened to them or their family in the year of the penny.

⑥ Ultimate Birthday Party

(Grade 6–Adult)

Ask students to dream a little about what their *ultimate* birthday party would be like? What would they eat, who would they invite, who would be the band? Have them share in small groups or to the class.

⑥ Brush With Celebrity

(Grade 5–Adult)

Ask students to share a time that they have had a brush with a celebrity. It could be a television star they saw at a theme park, or a sports figure they met at a game, and so forth.

CONTEMPORARY VARIATIONS

With the advent of the World Wide Web, e-mail, text messaging, iPod, and other technological innovations, we must be aware of the latest trends and be able to take advantage of them to build rapport with our students. The following activities are examples of this.

⑥ What's On Your iPod?

(Grade 3–Adult)

Students tell classmates what is, or what they would ultimately like, on their iPod.

⑥ Quote This!

(Grade 6–Adult)

Many people add a quote under their e-mail signature. Ask students what they would use. You could give students a week to create or find a quote, or give them a list of 10 or so quotes, ranging from profound to funny, and ask them to choose.

⊚ Missing Links

(Grade 6–Adult)

In these days of the World Wide Web, many people have their own homepage. Ask students what Web sites they would link to their homepage. The Web sites (real or imagined) and the reasons why they are important to the student are shared in large or small groups.

GROUP CHALLENGES

Social cooperation is intrinsically rewarding for the human brain (Rilling et al., 2002). Having students participate in group challenges such as the ones listed here can help increase their sense of community by emphasizing the group instead of the individual, making the classroom a friendlier, less threatening, place to be.

⊚ Debriefings

(Grade 3–Adult)

These are fun activities that can stand alone as team-building activities or state changes. However, any kind of experiential activity such as this can be so much richer in insight, education, and self-discovery if the teacher can lead a debriefing discussion after the activity. The easiest debrief framework I have ever used is down to two questions that the teacher asks the students:

1. What happened?

The teacher facilitates a discussion about what happened from the student's perspective. Was it difficult? Did you think you were going to give up? What was frustrating about the experience? How did it feel when it was done? This is the time to share whatever happened to the students physically or mentally during the activity.

2. How is that like life?

The teacher can facilitate a discussion about the connections between this activity and life. Does everything in life make sense? Do we sometimes have to make the best of a tough situation? Do things sometimes seem frustrating but if we stick with them, it was all worth it? These activities are very rich lessons for members of the group to learn about one another, and for individuals to learn about themselves.

☺ Liszt List

(Grade 4–Adult)

Have students break into groups and challenge them to do one of the following tasks in one minute:

+ List as many composers as they can (i.e., Liszt, Beethoven, etc.).
+ List as many Disney characters as they can.
+ List as many Dr. Seuss books as they can.
+ List as many brands of soap (hand soap, dish soap, etc.) as they can.
+ List as many words as they can with double letters (i.e., moon, rubble, etc.).
+ This could be a fun way to review as well, asking students to list as many types of geometric figures as they can, as many Spanish verbs as they can, as many pieces of classical music as they can, and so on.
+ Add to this list with your own curriculum, style, and imagination.

☺ Alphabet Find

(Grade 5–Adult)

Put students in pairs or small groups no bigger than four and hand each of them a sheet of paper with the letters of the alphabet written in order, top to bottom.

Challenge the groups to think of one thing for each letter, a thing that relates to the course or subject. For example, in a literature class, a group could write metaphor for "M."

The first group to complete the alphabet or the group that uses the most letters wins.

+ Vary the activity by making it a team-building exercise. Have the groups find an object for every letter of the alphabet, using only what they have at their desks, including the contents of their purses, pockets, wallets, notebooks, and backpacks. Accept any creative answer they can sufficiently justify.
+ Have students come up with alphabetical lists of different things, for example, a shopping list A to Z, a list of restaurants, and so on.

At the end of the activity, have group members share a few of the more clever or creative items they came up with.

⑤ Life Raft

(Grade 5–Adult)

1. Students get into groups of five to eight.

2. Students stand shoulder to shoulder in a tight circle facing the center of the circle.

3. One person from each group goes to the instructor to get one 11-by-14 sheet of construction paper.

4. Groups are challenged to find a way for each of their members to fit onto the paper, so that no part of any group member is touching the floor.

5. The groups must hold the position until the teacher can verify that they accomplished their goal. Creativity is greatly encouraged to showcase the numerous ways this task can be accomplished.

6. When all groups have successfully met the challenge, instruct the groups to pick up the paper, fold it in half, short end to short end and repeat! You can also challenge the students to see which group can reach the goal on the smallest piece of paper.

⊚ Turn the Page
(Grade 6–Adult)

This is very fun, and can be pretty high gradient, so I wouldn't do this until the group members are pretty comfortable with one another. A flat object, such as a sheet, a towel, a garbage bag, is laid on the floor. A team of students, anywhere between four and eight, depending on the size of the object, are asked to stand on the sheet and, without stepping off the sheet, flip the sheet over so all are standing on the other side.

⊚ Yurt Circle
(Grade 3–Adult)

A *yurt* is a portable dwelling made of branches and felt, used by the nomadic tribes of Mongolia. Use this as a lesson about group dynamics and relying on one another.

1. The entire class stands in a circle, facing the center.

2. Students number off. There must be an even number of participants. (The teacher can join in if need be.)

3. Verify that students know if they are an odd or even number, by having the "odds" raise their hands, then the "evens."

4. Everyone in the circle holds hands.

5. Very slowly, being aware of the changing dynamics of the group, the evens slowly and fluidly lean in toward the center of the circle, and the odds lean back, out of the circle. All students keep their feet on the floor.

6. Reverse the roles a few times so everyone can feel the shift of balance and motion.

◉ Group Untie

(Grade 4–Adult)

1. Students get into groups of five to eight.

2. Each group stands in a tight circle, shoulder to shoulder, facing the middle of the circle.

3. Students reach in and grab someone else's hand with their right hand, and a different hand with their left hand, creating a jumble of hands and arms in the middle of the circle.

4. At a signal from the teacher, the groups begin to untie the knot without letting go of each other's hands.

5. When members of a group successfully untie themselves, allow them to celebrate with a cheer or by waving their clasped hands.

◉ I've Got My Eye on You

(Grade 4–Adult)

1. Students stand facing in a circle of six to eight members.

2. One student is chosen to be the leader. The leader's job is to say, "Go" and keep score.

3. To begin the game, everyone looks down at the floor.

4. When the leader says, "Go," everyone looks up at one of the other group members and holds the gaze.

5. If two people have made eye contact with each other, the group gets a point. If there is no eye contact, then no point.

6. Continue until one of the groups scores 10 points.

◎ Eye See You

(Grade 4–Adult)

1. In partners, one person (A) shuts his eyes, and the other partner (B) looks at one of A's closed eyes.

2. Partner A decides, behind closed lids, which of B's eyes to look into when he open his eyes.

3. When ready, B tells A to open his eyes. When A opens his eyes, if B is looking at the eye that A is looking at, B gets a point. Game continues for 5 points.

◎ Fast Fingers

(Grade 4–Adult)

1. Students choose a partner and decide who will go first.

2. Partners stand back to back.

3. Give the class a specific math operation, like subtraction or multiplication, to use during the play of this game.

4. The first partner creates a math problem using the designated math operation, and displays the problem on the fingers of both hands. Tell students they are limited to numbers of five or less, and will represent zero with a fist. For example, if doing an addition problem, five fingers on one hand and four on the other would signify the addition problem 5 + 4.

5. At your cue, the partners turn around to face each other.

6. The first partner displays the math problem and the second partner must solve it and say the answer within the time limit you set (the time depends on the skill of the participants, but should be equal for all). The first partner must verify that the answer is correct and provide the correct answer if it is not.

7. Partners turn back to back again and the second partner devises a math problem for the first partner to solve at the next cue.
  - Variation: Have partners stand back to back, and on the signal turn to face each other with each displaying a number of fingers, from zero to 10. The students then race to see which partner can do the math problem presented, whether addition, subtraction, or multiplication. The first partner to figure out the answer shouts it out.

◎ One Object Touch

(Grade 5–Adult)

I would not do this activity until a firm community of high support and low threat has been established. The teacher simply puts out an object, such as a piece of paper, and asks that students arrange themselves so they are all touching the object. The fun comes in as the teacher makes the object smaller and smaller (but still within the realm of success for the students).

JUST FOR FUN

To create the optimal learning environment, the teacher should strive to create an atmosphere of high challenge, high support, and low threat. Few things are as effective as laughter in reducing stress hormones, improving mood, enhancing creativity, reducing pain, improving immunity, and lowering blood pressure.

Humor, whether intentional or spontaneous, can help reduce a sense of threat in the classroom environment. A recent study of 300 university students found that teachers who used humor in the classroom were perceived as more human, more approachable, and more motivating than instructors who did not use humor (Wanzer & Frymier, 1999).

Laughter increases the amount of oxygen in the blood, thus stimulating the brain. Laughter and a good sense of humor have long been known to reduce stress, and stress reduction decreases the risk of ailments such as heart disease and has been shown to improve the outcomes of many health interventions (Hassed, 2001). Humor may also boost the immune system. A recent study (Bennett, Zeller, Rosenberg, & McCann, 2003) showed that the greater the amount of mirthful laughter exhibited by a patient, the greater the increase in that patients' immune function.

Even a simple activity like telling a joke can be good for your brain. Telling and understanding a joke involves many parts of the brain, including working memory, cognitive shifting (because jokes require you to look at familiar things from a new angle), abstract reasoning, and language cognition. Studies have shown that telling or understanding a good joke provides the brain with an invigorating mental workout because so many parts of the brain are stimulated (Shammi & Stuss, 1999).

This final section includes some unusual activities, such as lighting a pickle and some magic tricks. My experience has been that these activities engender curiosity. What a great state in which to be in a classroom!

Any discussion of curiosity must begin with Daniel Berlyne, considered to be the seminal mind in the study of curiosity. His neurophysiological view associated curiosity with exploratory behavior. He identified two forms of exploratory behavior, diversive (e.g., seeking relief from boredom) and specific (e.g., uncertainty, conceptual conflict). It is specific curiosity that is of most interest to educators. Berlyne described specific exploration in the context of epistemic curiosity, that is, "the brand of arousal that motivates the quest for knowledge and is relieved when knowledge is procured" (Berlyne, 1960, p. 274). Unusual and even silly activities such as the state changes in this section could certainly be used to arouse the parts of the brain that would increase students' curiosity in the classroom.

With all of these potential benefits, why wouldn't you try to intentionally introduce humor into your classroom?

⑥ Classic Dance

(K–Adult)

Put on some old favorites and see what happens. Chicken Dance, The Limbo, The Twist, Bunny Hop, Hokey Pokey. Why not? This could be fun and has the added benefit of repetitive movement of gross-motor muscles that will increase dopamine levels and help students feel good.

⑥ 60-Second Joke Time

(Grade 2–Adult)

The psychological and physiological benefits of laughter have already been discussed. Here are some other ways to intentionally introduce humor into the classroom.

+ After setting the parameters for what is an acceptable joke, give students 60 seconds at their tables to share a joke. When finished, ask for volunteers to share jokes with the entire group.
+ Ask volunteers to be ready to share their jokes some other day, when a joke break is needed.
+ With a partner or in small groups, have students share a funny, unusual, or just bizarre event that has happened to them in their life. You could have student volunteers share with the entire class some especially interesting stories.

⑥ The Art Show

(Grade 4–Adult)

1. Students stand and find a partner.

2. One partner is designated "A," the other partner "B."

3. A is the artist; B slumps over at the waist, and becomes a lump of clay.

4. A moves B into strange positions to create a sculpture out of B.

5. When done, B's stay in their new sculpted state while all A's in the room go to the art show, and admire the sculptures there.

6. Switch. B's become the artists, A's become the lumps of clay.

   • Variation: After everyone has had a turn at being both the artist and the lump of clay, have pairs combine into groups of four or six, and have several lumps and several artists.

   • Remind them that they can have kinetic sculptures too (kinetic sculptures move!).

⑤ The Student Circus

(Grade 3–Adult)

Have students think of anything unique they would be willing to show or do for the group (e.g., double-jointed, rolling tongue, a difficult or popular dance step, the ability to wiggle their ears, etc.).

Make a list of volunteers with these unusual abilities, and have them perform at various intervals when a state change is needed throughout the semester or course.

⑤ Light a Pickle

(K–Adult)

Warning!!! This is a stunt for the teacher to do!! Do not allow students to try this!

Yeah, light a pickle. It actually works. If you have never done this, you are in for quite a surprise. It requires some pre-class at-home preparation with a few simple tools from a hardware store, but it's worth it.

1. Get a large dill pickle.

2. Get a small extension cord, like the lightweight ones used to plug in holiday lights.

3. With a wire cutter, cut off the female end of the plug, then strip the plastic back so that an inch or so of the bare wire is showing.

4. Get two 16D nails, and wrap one wire of the extension cord around each nail.

5. Wrap up the exposed wire with electrical tape. Your extension cord should now have a plug at one end and two nails wrapped with wire and a bundle of wires wrapped with electrical tape at the other end.

6. Push a nail into each end of the pickle, making sure the nails do not touch.

7. Turn off the lights in the classroom, hold the pickle with rubber-tipped tongs, and plug the cord into an outlet with regular 110V household current. Do not touch the nails while the cord is plugged into the wall.

8. Ooh and ahh as you watch the pickle glow.
   - Note: It may take a few seconds for the pickle to start glowing.
   - Another note: It will eventually start to smoke, and may smell a little, but don't let that stop you from getting the thrill of a lifetime!

☉ The Chicken Break

(Grade 4–Adult)

1. Get a dishtowel and lay it down long-ways in front of you.

2. Roll each short side so you have two rolls meet in the center.

3. Pick up the two rolls, and flip them over so the opening is facing down.

4. Fold the towel in half with the opening on the outside, so it looks like four rolls at the top edge.

5. Look down at the four rolls. Reach into each roll and pull out just a little bit of the corner in the middle of

each roll. Grab the protruding corners of the left two rolls with one hand, and

6. Hold on to two opposite corners, pause dramatically, and say "chicken" while pulling the corners away from each other.

☉ Cheesy Magic—The Disappearing Leg

(K–Adult)

Kids love magic, kids love cheese—put them together, and you have some of the cheesiest magic tricks ever invented! These are magic tricks so cheesy that they will extract a groan—and a grin—from even your toughest audiences. You the teacher could perform any of these, or you could break the class into groups, teach each group a different trick, and have them perform for one another.

Speaking of cheesy magic tricks, the disappearing leg trick is one of them. The teacher stands in front of the class, and holds a towel, or perhaps a sports coat, covering his legs.

1. The teacher lifts the sports coat up, showing both legs.

2. The teacher moves the sports coat back down, covering the legs.

3. While the legs are covered, the teacher bends one leg up at the knee.

4. The sports coat is again lifted, showing that one leg has apparently disappeared!

5. The sports coat is moved back down, covering up the legs.

6. The leg is put back down on the floor.

7. The sports coat is lifted again to reveal the restored leg, much to the relief of the audience.

☉ Cheesy Magic—Crazy Fingers

(Grade 3–Adult)

The effect is that the students' palms are together, yet a stray finger is wiggling both above and below the hands.

1. Palms are placed together

2. Both middle fingers are bent forward

3. Keeping the fingers bent, the palms are rotated 180 degrees, the hand on top rotating counter-clockwise, the hand on the bottom rotating in a clockwise direction.

4. Wiggle the middle fingers—the illusion is complete!

☉ Cheesy Magic—The Amazing *Growing* Arm

(K–Adult)

The effect—the teacher pulls on her arm and it "magically" grows several inches.

1. One arm is straightened out in front of you, elbow locked.

2. Move that shoulder back as far as you can go.

3. Tug the end of the sleeve of your suit jacket or sweater as far forward as you can, over the extended arm.

4. Stand sideways with your extended arm away from the audience.

5. With your free hand, grab the wrist of the extended arm, and pull.

6. While pulling, move shoulder forward. Do this slowly and with some effort for the proper effect.

☺ Cheesy Magic—The Amazing *Shrinking* Arm

(Grade 4–Adult)

The body responds psychologically and physiologically to both real and perceived threats in the classroom or in life. When threat is perceived, students downshift to the more primitive areas of the brain in control of brute survival and are unable to freely access the neocortex, which is essential for new learning. This activity can be used as a springboard for many discussions, such as the effect of stress on the body or the physical effect of psychologically tense moments, like when one student has been put down or insulted by another.

1. All students stand facing a wall, just close enough so that when they lift an arm out toward the wall, their fingertips barely brush the wall.

2. Without moving away from the wall, have students make a fist with one hand, bend their arm in a right angle and squeeze and tense their arm muscles for a count of 10.

3. When they are done counting, the teacher instructs the students to again reach out toward the wall, noting how much their arms have "shrunk" in such a short time.

4. Without moving away from the wall, have students relax their arms and shake the tension out of the arm muscles and reach for the wall again. They will notice that the arm has lengthened back to its original size.

☺ The Pen Twist

(Grade 4–Adult)

This is not a magic trick, just a particular way to move your hands.

1. Hold hands with palms together.

2. Place a pen in the crook between thumbs and forefingers.

3. With the fingers of the left hand, reach over the pointer finger of your right hand and grab the pen.

4. Cross your left thumb over your right thumb.

5. The next two moves happen at the same time: With the fingers of your left hand, grab the pen and pull along the length of your right pointer finger. At the same time, your right thumb pushes the other end of the pen around your left thumb.

6. The ending position is with your hands side by side, pointer fingers touching, both palms facing away from you, with the pen in the crook of the thumbs.

7. Once you master the trick this way, try to reverse it, and start with the pen in front of your palms, and move it around to the back.

References

Ackerman, S. (1992). *Discovering the brain*. Washington, DC: National Academy Press.

Adamson, G., O'Kane, D., & Shevlin, M. (2005). Students' ratings of teaching effectiveness: A laughing matter? *Psychological Reports, 96*(1), 225–226.

Alden, D. L., Mukherjee, A., & Hoyer, W. D. (2000). The effects of incongruity, surprise and positive moderators on perceived humor in television advertising. *Journal of Advertising, 29*(2), 1–16.

Anders, C., & Berg, C. A. R. (2005). Factors related to observed attitude change toward learning chemistry among university students. *Chemistry Education Research & Practice, 6*(1), 1–18.

Ariel, G. (1978). Computerized dynamic resistive exercise. In F. Landry & W. A. R. Orban (Eds.), *Mechanics of sports and kinanthropometry* (Book 6, pp. 45–51). Miami, FL: Symposia Specialists.

Ashcraft, M. H., & Kirk, E. P. (2001). The relationships among working memory, math anxiety, and performance. *Journal of Experimental Psychology: General, 130*, 224–237.

Bennett, M. P., Zeller, J. M., Rosenberg, L., & McCann, J. (2003). The effect of mirthful laughter on stress and natural killer cell activity. *Alternative Therapies in Health and Medicine, 9*(2), 38–45.

Berg, C. A. R. (2005). *Learning chemistry at the university level: Student attitudes, motivation, and design of the learning environment.* Unpublished doctoral dissertation, Umeå University, Sweden.

Berlyne, D. E. (1960). *Conflict, arousal, and curiosity.* New York: McGraw-Hill.

Bernardi, L., Wdowczyk-Szulc, J., Valenti, C., Castoldi, S., Passino, C., Spadacini, G., & Sleight, P. (2000). Effects of controlled breathing, mental activity and mental stress with or without verbalization on heart rate variability. *Journal of American College of Cardiology, 35*, 1462–1469.

Berninger, V., & Rutberg, J. (1992). Relationship of finger function to beginning writing: Application to diagnosis of writing disabilities. *Developmental Medicine and Child Neurology, 34*, 198–215.

Berns, G. S., Cohen, J. D., & Mintun, M. A. (1997). Brain regions responsive to novelty in the absence of awareness. *Science, 276,* 1272–1275.

Birnbaum, M. H. (1993). Vision disorders frequently interfere with reading and learning. *Journal of Behavioral Optometry, 4*(3), 66, 69–71.

Bischoff-Grethe, A., Martin, M., Mao, H., & Berns, G. S. (2001). The context of uncertainty modulates the subcortical response to predictability. *Journal of Cognitive Neuroscience, 13,* 986–993.

Blaydes, J. (2001). *How to make learning a moving experience.* Richardson, TX: Action Based Learning.

Blood, A. J., & Zatorre, R. J. (2001). Intensely pleasurable responses to music correlate with activity in brain regions implicated in reward and emotion. *Proceedings of the National Academy of Science, 98*(20), 11818–11823.

Botwinick, J. (1997). *Developing musical/rhythmic intelligence to improve spelling skills.* Master's project, Kean College, Union, NJ.

Burnett, K. M., Solterbeck, L. A., & Strapp, C. M. (2004). Scent and mood state following an anxiety-provoking task. *Psychological Reports, 95,* 707–722.

Burns, L. H., Annett, L., Kelley, A. E., Everitt, B. J., & Robbins, T. W. (1996). Effects of lesions to amygdala, ventral subiculum, medial prefrontal cortex and nucleus accumbens on the reaction to novelty: Implications for limbic-striatal interactions. *Behavioral Neuroscience, 110,* 60–73.

Burns, R. A. (1985). *Information impact and factors affecting recall.* Paper presented at the annual National Conference on Teaching Excellence and Conference of Administrators, Austin, TX. (ERIC Document Reproduction Service No. ED258639)

Cahill, L., & McGaugh, J. L. (1998). Mechanisms of emotional arousal and lasting declarative memory. *Trends in Neuroscience, 21,* 294–299.

Caine, G., Caine, R. N., & Crowell, S. (1999). MindShifts: A brain-compatible process for professional development and the renewal of education. Tucson, AZ: Zephyr Press.

Calvin, W. H. (1996). *How brains think.* New York: Basic Books.

Canfield, J., & Hansen, M. V. (1993). *Chicken soup for the soul: 101 stories to open the heart and rekindle the spirit.* Deerfield Beach, FL: Health Communications.

Case-Smith, J., & Pehoski, C. (Eds.). (1992). *Development of hand skills in the child.* Bethesda, MD: American Occupational Therapy Association.

Christakis, D. A., Zimmerman, F., DiGiuseppe, D., & McCarty, C. (2004). Early television exposure and subsequent attentional problems in children. *Pediatrics, 113*(4), 708–713.

Cockerton, T., Moore, S., & Norman, D. (1997). Cognitive test performance and background music. *Perceptual and Motor Skills, 85,* 1435–1438.

Dennison, P. (1989). *The brain gym.* Ventura, CA: Edu-Kinesthetics.

DePorter, B. (1992). *Quantum learning.* New York: Dell.

Diamond, M. C. (1988). *Enriching heredity: The impact of the environment on the anatomy of the brain.* New York: Free Press.

Diamond, M. C., & Hopson, J. (1998). *Magic trees of the mind.* New York: Dutton.

Diego, M. A., Jones, N. A., Field, T., Hernandez-Reif, M., Schanberg, S., Kuhn, C., et al. (1998). Aromatherapy positively affects mood, EEG patterns of alertness and math computations. *International Journal of Neuroscience, 96*(3/4), 217–224.

Druckman, D., & Sweets, J. (1988). *Enhancing human performance: Issues, theories, and techniques.* Englewood Cliffs, NJ: Prentice Hall.

Duffee, R. A., & Koontz, R. (1965). Behavioral effects of ionized air on rats. *Psychophysiology, 1*(4), 347–359.

Erecinska, M., & Silver, I. (2001). Tissue oxygen tension and brain sensitivity to hypoxia. *Respiration Physiology, 128*(3), 263–276.

Featherstone, H. (Ed.). (1986, September). Cooperative learning. *Harvard Education Letter,* pp. 4–6.

Feehan, M., McGee, R., Williams, S. M., & Nada-Raja, S. (1995). Models of adolescent psychopathology: Childhood risk and the transition to adulthood. *Journal of the American Academy of Child and Adolescent Psychiatry, 34*(5), 670–679.

Fisher, A. G. (1991). Vestibular-proprioceptive processing and bilateral integration and sequencing deficits. In A. G. Fisher, E. A. Murray, & A. C. Bundy (Eds.), *Sensory integration theory and practice* (pp. 71–72, 77). Philadelphia: F. A. Davis Company.

Flapper, B. C., Houwen, S., & Schoemaker, M. M. (2006). Fine motor skills and effects of methylphenidate in children with attention-deficit-hyperactivity disorder and developmental coordination disorder. *Developmental Medicine and Child Neurology, 48*(3), 165–169.

Fletcher, P. C., Shallice, T., & Dolan, R. J. (1998). The functional roles of the prefrontal cortex in episodic memory. *Brain, 121,* 1239–1248.

Gagné, R. M. (1985). *The conditions of learning and theory of instruction.* Fort Worth, TX: Holt, Rinehart & Winston.

Glasser, W. (1986). *Control theory in the classroom.* New York: Perennial Library.

Goetz, E. T., & Sadoski, M. (1996). Imaginative processes in literary comprehension: Bringing the text to life. In R. J. Kreuz & M. S. MacNealy (Eds.), *Empirical approaches to the study of literature and aesthetics* (pp. 221–240). Norwood, NJ: Ablex.

Grossman, E., Grossman, A., Schein, M. H., Zimlichman, R., & Gavish, B. (2001). Breathing-control lowers blood pressure. *Journal of Human Hypertension, 15*, 263–269.

Gully, S. M., Payne, S. C., Kiechel Koles, K. L., & Whiteman, J. A. (2002). The impact of error-training and individual differences on training outcomes: An attribute-treatment interaction perspective. *Journal of Applied Psychology, 87*(1), 143–155.

Guy, S. C., & Cahill, L. (1999). The role of overt rehearsal in enhanced conscious memory for emotional events. *Conscious Cognition, 8*(1), 114–122.

Hall, L. M., & Belnap, B. P. (2002). *The sourcebook of magic*. Williston, VT: Crown House.

Han, S., Hur, M., Buckle, J., Choi, J., & Lee, M. (2006). Effects of aromatherapy on symptoms of dysmenorrhea in college students: A randomized placebo-controlled clinical trial. *Journal of Alternative Complementary Medicine, 12*, 535–541.

Hannaford, C. (1995). *Smart moves: Why learning is not all in your head*. Arlington, VA: Great Ocean Publishers.

Hart, L. (2002). *Human brain and human learning* (3rd ed.). New York: Books for Educators.

Hassed, C. (2001). How humour keeps you well. *Australian Family Physician, 30*(1), 25–28.

Hastings, N., & Wood, K. C. (2002). *Reorganizing primary classroom learning*. Buckingham, UK: Open University Press.

Hatfield, T., & McGaugh, J. L. (1999). Norepinephrine infused into the basolateral amygdala posttraining enhances retention in a spatial water maze task. *Neurobiology of Learning and Memory, 71*, 232–239.

Hathaway, W. E., Hargreaves, J. A., Thompson, G. W., & Novitsky, D. (1992). *A study into the effects of light on children of elementary school age: A case of daylight robbery*. Edmonton, Canada: Alberta Education.

Hawkins, L. H., & Barker, T. (1978). Air ions and human performance. *Ergonomics, 21*(4), 273–278.

Heiervang, E., & Hugdahl, K. (2003). Impaired visual attention in children with dyslexia. *Learning Disabilities, 36*(1), 68–73.

Heschong Mahone Group. (1999). *Daylighting in schools: An investigation into the relationship between daylighting and human performance* (Report No. HMG-R-9803). (ERIC Document Reproduction Service No. ED444337)

Hirschi, T. (1969). *The causes of delinquency*. Berkeley: University of California Press.

Hoffman, L. G. (1980). Incidence of vision difficulties in children with learning disabilities. *Journal of the American Optometrist Association, 51*(5), 447–451.

Holloway, J. (2000). Extracurricular activities: The path to academic success? *Educational Leadership, 57,* 4.

Imura, M., Misao, H., & Ushijima, H. (2006). The psychological effects of aromatherapy-massage in healthy postpartum mothers. *Journal of Midwifery & Women's Health, 51,* 21–27.

Jacobs, B. L., & Fornal, C. A. (1997). Serotonin and motor activity. *Current Opinion in Neurobiology, 7*(6), 820–825.

Jacobs, W. J., & Nadel, L. (1985). Stress-induced recovery of fears and phobias. *Psychological Review, 92,* 512–531.

James, W. (1980). *Writings from 1878 to 1899: Psycholgy/Briefer course/The will to believe/Talks to teachers and students/Essays* (G. E. Myers, Ed.). New York: The Library of America.

Jensen, E. (2000). *Learning with the body in mind.* San Diego, CA: The Brain Store.

Johnstone, A. H., & Percival, F. (1976). Attention breaks in lectures. *Education in Chemistry, 13,* 49–50.

Klein, H. J., & Kim, J. S. (1998). A field study of the influence of situational constraints, leader-member exchange and goal commitment on performance. *Academy of Management Journal, 41,* 88–95.

Klein, R., Pilon, D., Prosser, S., & Shannahoff-Khalsa, D. (1986). Nasal airflow asymmeteries and human performance. *Biological Psychology, 23,* 127–137.

Koester, C. (2001). The effect of brain gym on reading abilities. *Brain Gym Journal, 15.* Available from http://www.braingym.org.

Kranowitz, C., Szklut, S., Balzer-Martin, L., Haber, E., & Sava, D. (2001). *Answers to questions teachers ask about sensory integration: Forms, checklists and practical tools for teachers and parents.* Las Vegas, NV: Sensory Resources.

Langer, J. A. (2001). Succeeding against the odds in English. *English Journal, 91*(1), 37–42.

Langleben, D., Austin, G., Goris, M., & Strauss, H. W. (2001). Evaluation of right/left asymmetries in regional cortical blood flow in prepubescent boys with attention deficit hyperactivity disorder. *Nuclear Medicine Communications, 22*(12), 1333–1340.

Ledoux, J. (1996). *The emotional brain.* New York: Simon & Schuster.

Leggio, M., Molinari, M., Neri, P., Graziano, A., Mandolesi, L., & Petrosini, L. (2000). Representation of actions in rats: The role of cerebellum in learning spatial performances by observation. *Neurobiology, 97*(5), 2320–2325.

Lehrner, J., Marwinski, G., Lehr, S., Johren, P., & Deecke, L. (2005). Ambient odors of orange and lavender reduce anxiety and improve mood in a dental office. *Physiology of Behavior, 86,* 92–95.

Leshchinskaia, I. S., Makarchuk, N. M., Lebeda, A. F., Krivenko, V. V., & Sgibnev, A. K. (1983). Effects of phytoncides on the dynamics of the cerebral circulation in flight controllers during their occupational activity. *Kosmicheskaia Biologiia i Aviakosmicheskaia Meditsina, 17*(2), 80–83.

Levinthal, C. (1988). *Messengers of paradise: Opiates and the brain: The struggle over pain, rage, uncertainty, and addiction.* New York: Anchor/Doubleday.

Lewith, G. T., Godfrey, A. D., & Prescott, P. (2005). A single-blinded, randomized pilot study evaluating the aroma of Lavandula augustifolia as a treatment for mild insomnia. *Journal of Alternative Complementary Medicine, 11,* 631–637.

MacElveen-Hoehn, P., & Eyres, S. J. (1984). Social support and vulnerability: State of the art in relation to families and children. *Birth Defects Original Article Series, 20*(5), 11–43.

McBride, C. M., Curry, S. J., Cheadle, A., Anderman, C., Wagner, E. H., & Diehr, P. (1995). School-level application of a social bonding model to adolescent risk-taking behavior. *Journal of School Health, 65*(2), 63–68.

McHale, K., & Cermak, S. (1992). Fine motor activities in elementary school: Preliminary findings and provisional implications for children with fine motor problems. *American Journal of Occupational Therapy, 46*(10), 898–903.

Miles, J. A., & Klein, H. J. (1998). The fairness of assigning group members to tasks. *Group and Organization Management, 23,* 71–96.

Miller, M. (2000). *Laughter is good for your heart.* Baltimore: University of Maryland Medical Center.

Morton, L. L., & Kershner, J. R. (1984). Negative air ionization improves memory and attention in learning-disabled and mentally retarded children. *Journal of Abnormal Child Psychology, 12*(2), 353–365.

Oleson, T. (2002). Auriculotherapy stimulation for neuro-rehabilitation. *NeuroRehabilitation 17,* 49–62.

Palmer, L. (1980). Auditory discrimination through vestibulo-cochlear stimulation. *Academic Therapy, 16*(1), 55–70.

Peyton, J. L., Bass, W. T., Burke, B. L., & Frank, L. M. J. (2005). Novel motor and somatosensory activity is associated with increased cerebral cortical blood volume measured by near-infrared optical topography. *Child Neurology, 20*(10), 817–821.

Piek, J. P., Baynam, G. B., & Barrett, N. C. (2006). The relationship between fine and gross motor ability, self-perceptions and self worth in children and adolescents. *Human Movement Science, 25*(1), 65–75.

Rauscher, F. H., Shaw, G. L., & Ky, K. N. (1993). Music and spatial task performance. *Nature, 365,* 611.

Rilling, J. K., Gutman, D. A., Zeh, T. R., Pagnoni, G., Berns, G. S., & Kilts, C. D. (2002). A neural basis for social cooperation. *Neuron, 35,* 395–405.

Ross, J. G., & Pate, R. R. (1987). The national children and youth fitness study II: A summary of findings. *Journal of Physical Education, Recreation and Dance, 58,* 51–56.

Schmidt, S. R. (1994). Effects of humor on sentence memory. *Journal of Experimental Psychology, 20*(4), 953–967.

Shammi, P., & Stuss, D. T. (1999). Humour appreciation: A role of the right frontal lobe. *Brain, 122*(4), 657–666.

Shannahoff-Khalsa, D. S., Boyle, M. R., & Buebel, M. E. (1991). The effects of unilateral forced nostril breathing on cognition. *International Journal of Neuroscience, 57*(3/4), 239–249.

Shephard, R. J. (1997). Curricular physical activity and academic performance. *Pediatric Exercise Science, 9,* 113–126.

Shephard, R. J., Volle, M., Lavalee, M., LaBarre, R., Jequier, J. C., & Rajic, M. (1984). Required physical activity and academic grades: A controlled longitudinal study. In J. Limarinen & I. Valimaki (Eds.), *Children and sport* (pp. 58–63). Berlin: Springer-Verlag.

Simons-Morton, B. G., Crump, A. D., Haynie, D. L., & Saylor, K. E. (1999). Student-school bonding and adolescent problem behavior. *Health, 14*(1), 99–107.

Slavin, R. (1987, March) Cooperative learning: Can students help students learn? *Instructor,* pp. 74–78.

Small, R. V., & Arnone, M. P. (2000). *Turning kids on to research: The power of motivation.* Englewood, CO: Libraries Unlimited. (ERIC Document Reproduction Service No. ED439689)

Smits-Engelsman, B. C. M., Swinnen, S. P., & Duysens, J. (2004). Are graphomotor tasks affected by working in the contralateral hemispace in 6- to 10-year-old children? *Journal of Motor Control, 8*(4), 521–533.

Smits-Engelsman, B. C. M., Van Galen, G. P., & Michelis, C. G. J. (1995). Prevalence of poor handwriting and the validity of estimation of motor proficiency and handwriting performance by teachers. *Tijdschrift voor Onderwijsresearch, 20,* 1–15.

Sousa, D. (2001). *How the brain learns* (2nd ed.). Reston, VA: National Association of Secondary School Principals.

Sowell, E. R., Thompson, P. M., Holmes, C. J., Jernigan, T. L., & Toga, A. W. (1999). In-vivo evidence for post-adolescent brain maturation in frontal and striatal regions. *Neuroscience, 2,* 859–861.

Stahl, R. J. (1990). *Using think-time behaviors to promote students' information processing, learning, and on task participation: An instructional module.* Tempe: Arizona State University. (ERIC Documentation Reproduction Service No. ED370885)

Sturm, Brian. (1999, July). The enchanted imagination: Storytelling's power to entrance listeners. *School Library Media Research, 2.* Available from http://www.ala.org/aasl/SLMR/slmr toc.html.

Sylvester, P. S. (1994). Elementary school curricula and urban transformation. *Harvard Educational Review, 64*(3), 309–331.

Symons, C. W., Cinelli, B., James, T. C., & Groff, P. (1997). Bridging student health risks and academic achievement through comprehensive school health programs. *Journal of School Health, 67*(6), 220–227.

Thompson, R. F., & Kim, J. J. (1981). Memory systems in the brain and localization of a memory. *Proceedings of the National Academy of Science, 93,* 13438–13444.

Tims, F., Clair, A. A., Cohen, D., Eisdorder, C., Koga, M., Kumar, A., et al. (1999, April). Paper presented at Music Medicine: Enhancing Health Through Music, Miami, FL.

Tithof, W. (1998). *Lighting spectrum effects on mood and vision in elementary school vision.* Stamford, CT: Verilux.

Tom, G., Poole, M. F., Galla, J., & Berrier, J. (1981). The influence of negative air ions on human performance and mood. *Human Factors, 23*(5), 633–636.

Tulving, E., Markowitsch, H. J., Craik, F. I. M., Habib, R., & Houle, S. (1996). Novelty and familiarity activations in PET studies of memory encoding and retrieval. *Cerebral Cortex, 6,* 71–79.

Turner, J. C., Midgley, C., Meyer, D. K., Gheen, M., Anderman, E. M., Kang, Y., & Patrick, H. (2002). The classroom environment and students' reports of avoidance strategies in mathematics: A multimethod study. *Journal of Educational Psychology, 94*(1), 88–106.

Vance, C. M. (1987). A comparative study on the use of humor in the design of instruction. *Instructional Science, 16*(1), 79–100.

van Driel, K. S., & Talling, J. C. (2005). Familiarity increases consistency in animal tests. *Behavioral Brain Research, 159*(2), 243–245.

Van Praag, H., Christie, B. R., Sejnowski, T. J., & Gage, F. H. (1999). Running enhances neurogenesis, learning and long-term potentiation in mice. *Proceedings of the National Academy of Science, 96,* 13427–13431.

Van Praag, H., Kempermann, G., & Gage, F. H. (1999). Running increases cell proliferation and neurogenesis in the adult mouse dentate gyrus. *Natural Neuroscience, 2,* 266–270.

Wanzer, M. B., & Frymier, A. B. (1999). The relationship between student perceptions of instructor humor and students' reports of learning. *Communication Education, 48*(1), 48–62.

Weitzberg, E., & Lundberg, J. O. N. (2002). Humming greatly increases nasal nitric oxide. *American Journal of Respiratory and Critical Care Medicine, 166,* 144–145.

Woodcock, E. A., & Richardson, R. (2000). Effects of environmental enrichment on rate of contextual processing and discriminative ability in adult rats. *Neurobiology of Learning and Memory, 73,* 1–10.

The Corwin Press logo—a raven striding across an open book—represents the union of courage and learning. Corwin Press is committed to improving education for all learners by publishing books and other professional development resources for those serving the field of PreK–12 education. By providing practical, hands-on materials, Corwin Press continues to carry out the promise of its motto: **"Helping Educators Do Their Work Better."**